Explorers

cooperative learning activities*

by Susan Schneck and Mary Strohl

*Lessons easily adaptable to traditional classroom or workstation settings

SCHOLASTIC
PROFESSIONAL BOOKS

New York • Toronto • London • Auckland • Sydney

About the Authors

Susan Schneck and Mary Strohl have many years' combined experience in education and publishing. In 1986 they started their own studio, Flights of Fancy, specializing in children's activity products and elementary teaching materials. This is their fourth title for Scholastic Professional Books.

Months of research have gone into making this book about explorers and their voyages to the Americas. We hope it is only a stepping stone, a beginning, to asking questions and finding more information in the myriad of books that are now available about the many cultures and traditions that make up our world.

special thanks to

Katherine Carson for her help in researching literature and classroom resources to teach about Native Peoples of the New World.

Mr. Isacco A. Valli, Assistant Director and Curator
Manitowoc Maritime Museum, Manitowoc, Wisconsin, for his suggestions
of navigation resources for the elementary classroom.

Robert Schneck for experimenting with cooperative learning
recipes in his classroom and sharing his experiences with us.
His insights illuminate, educate, and inspire!

ISBN 0-590-49232-2

Printed in the U.S.A.

CURR
E
101
.S36
1993

Table of Contents

Using the Activities in This Book

The purpose of this book is:
- To provide rich information on the voyages of 8 explorers from 1492 to 1700:
  Christopher Colombus (1492)   Hernan Cortés (1519)
  Hernando de Soto (1539)   Francisco Coronado (1593)
  Jacques Cartier (1535)   Samuel de Champlain (1603)
  Henry Hudson (1607)   Father Jacques Marquette, Louis Joliet (1673)
- To provide learning activities to help your students consider what it was like to be an adventurer as well as the Native Peoples of the explored lands.
- To help your students imagine the riches that drew the explorers across uncharted seas and discover the tools of navigation that helped them.
- To help you organize your classroom for using cooperative learning techniques with easy-to-follow guidelines.

Chapter one has a reproducible time line covering the centuries of European exploration we have included and other world events taking place at that time. Reproduce the time line following the instructions on page 5 prior to beginning group lessons. Subsequent chapters contain information and activities that will be added to the time line by cooperative groups. Introduce these materials prior to beginning group lessons. Look over the text and verify any unfamiliar vocabulary words you may need to introduce to your groups.

If you are unfamiliar with cooperative techniques, see the appendix in the back of the book for pointers and for a more detailed key to the recipe symbols shown with each lesson. **We have included charts, badges and other classroom helps keyed to the theme of this book.** Cooperative symbols at the beginning of each activity will tell you how to organize groups and how they will proceed. Beside the symbols social skills, academic skills, and teacher directions are provided.

See the appendix in the back of the book for:
- Cooperative learning overview and classroom guidelines
- Social skill descriptions and teaching techniques
- Cooperative recipe descriptions and symbols
- Reproducible classroom management charts and role badges
- Reproducible reward certificate

About This Book

The age of European explorers and navigators began long before Christopher Columbus set foot on the sands of what he called San Salvador in 1492. Leif Eriksson preceded him by almost five hundred years with his travels to Greenland and probably to the shores of what is now North America. During the eleventh and twelfth centuries thousands of crusaders traveled from all across Europe to the Middle East where they lost a fight for control of the Holy Land.

When the crusaders returned home to Europe, they brought many unfamiliar Eastern spices, silk material, and precious gems. The people of Europe wanted more of them. Jewels and silks made them rich. Spices made bland food taste better. Stronger ships were built to travel across long distances. New maps were drawn to show unknown lands. The printing press was invented in 1455. Books on navigation provided more people with the skills necessary to travel to the East and back again safely. Every country in Europe wanted to control trade with the East. Control would make them richer and more powerful than their neighbors. Daring seafaring men and navigators had been trying for years to find shorter, quicker routes to the East to trade for more goods.

This was the Europe where Columbus grew up. He and other sailors knew that the world was round. Columbus convinced Queen Isabella and King Ferdinand of Spain that he could sail straight west to Japan. He would bring them the riches of gold and spices that would make them the most powerful rulers in Europe.

No one in Europe in 1492 knew that two huge continents and another vast ocean blocked the way to the East. Columbus died believing his voyages west had brought him to Asia. It took decades of exploration for the kings and merchants of Europe to realize they were exploring lands they had not known had existed. They sent many explorers along their coasts, believing that there must be a sea route to the spices and riches they wanted. These explorers and navigators never found a short route to the East, but they did find many different cultures and new plants, foods, and animals. They brought these home to Europe. The more they explored, the more they wanted to know.

Europeans did not understand other cultures and their customs. Because the native peoples lived differently than Europeans, the exlorers thought of them as inferior to themselves. We now know that great cultures developed all over the world. Many of them were as impressive as Europe at the time, if not more so. Let's discard old stereotypes and learn from those who lived their lives in many different, but not inferior ways.

Ahoy, mates! Let's climb aboard ship and travel to faraway places. We're going to learn about these years of European sea travel by tagging along on several of the explorer's voyages. We'll get an idea of what it felt like to adventure to unknown places. We'll meet some of the people the brave explorers met. We'll learn about some of the tools that helped them cross the wide Atlantic and then got them home again. Let's discover what happens when different cultures get to know one another.

EXPLORATION RESOURCES

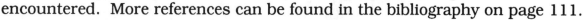

Following is a list of books, games, and other materials that will help your class learn more about the age of European exploration and some of the native peoples the explorers encountered. More references can be found in the bibliography on page 111.

1492 Year of Columbus by Genevieve Foster (Charles Scribner's Sons, 1969)

Columbus: Game in a Book by Mary Pearce (Scholastic Professional Books, 1992)

Directory of Columbus Quincentennial Projects by National Park Service and the Department of the Interior.

Discoverers of the New World by the editors of American Heritage (Harper and Row, 1960)

Discovering Christopher Columbus: How History is Invented by Kathy Pelta (Lerner Publications Company, Minneapolis, 1991)

Explorers Card Game (U. S. Games Systems, Inc., 1989)

First Encounters: Spanish Explorations in the Caribbean and U. S. editied by Jerold T. Milanich and Susan Milbrath (University of Florida Press, 1989)

The Life Treasury of American Folklore by Time, Inc. (1961)

The Log of Christopher Columbus translated by Robert H. Fuson (International Marine Publishing Co., 1987)

Pedro's Journal by Pam Conrad (Boyds Mills Press, 1991)

Ships and Seafarers: Tales of Ships and the Men Who Sailed in Them by Erik Abranson (Silver Burdett Company, 1980)

The Spice Adventure by Albert Barker (Julian Messner, no date)

Tales of Courage: Explorers of North America by Susan Baker (Steck-Vaughn Library, Austin Texas, 1989)

The Vikings by Robert Nicholson and Claire Watts (Scholastic, 1992)

Westward With Columbus by John Dyson (Scholastic/Madison Press, 1991)

The World of Columbus and Sons by Genevieve Foster (Charles Scribner's Sons, 1965)

EXPLORATION RESOURCES

Books About Native Peoples

Among the Volcanoes by Omar S. Casteneda (Dutton, 1991). When her mother becomes ill, Isabel, a Mayan girl living in contemporary Guatemala, must care for her and search for her own identity in a world fraught with upheaval and change.

The Ancient Maya by Barbara Beck (Franklin Watts, 1983). Discusses the Mayan culture, its discovery by the Spaniards, and its eventual collapse. Describes the ruins existing today.

A Civilization Project Book, Aztecs by Susan Purdy and Cass R. Sandak (Franklin Watts, 1982). Describes some of the achievements of Aztec civilization and includes instructions for reproducing Aztec masks, cloaks, drums, foods, etc.

The Creeks, Indians of North America by Michael D. Green (Chelsea House Publishers, 1990). Bibliographic references examining the culture, history, and changing fortunes of the Creek Indians.

Doctor Coyote, A Native American's Aesop's Fables by John Bierhorst (Macmillan Publishing Company, 1987). Coyote is featured in each of these Aztec Fables.

Indians of Mexico by Margaret C. Farquhar (Holt, Rinehart & Winston, 1967). Early migration across land bridge from Asia, through North America to Mexico. History of early Mexican Indians.

Moon Rope by Lois Ehlert (Harcourt Brace Javoanich, 1992). An adaptation of a Peruvian Inca Folktale in which Fox and Mole try to climb to the moon on a rope of woven grass. Illustrative of Indian folktales and myths similar to those of Aztec and Mayan cultures.

One Day in Aztec Mexico by G. B. Kirtland (Harcourt, Brace & World, Inc., 1983). Story of an upper middle-class Aztec family preparing for a celebration of a special event, the birth of a new baby.

Rain Player by David Wisniewski (Calrion Books, 1991). Pik challenges the rain god to a game of Pok-a-tok to bring rain to his thirsty Mayan village.

Spirit Child, A Story of the Nativity by John Bierhorst (William Morrow and Company, 1984). An English translation of the Aztec version of the birth of Christ told in 1583 by the Spaniards who had conquered the Aztecs.

Chapter 1
Spanning the Globe—An Exploration Time Line

After discussing the background material on page four with your class, group them to color and assemble the time line around the room. The time line and co-op activities provided in this chapter are not designed so that children simply memorize each date or event shown on the time line. It is meant to be used as a classroom reference point to help children visualize historical events in order, and to see how information and travel expanded during the time period we're describing.

The **Time Travelers** cards will help your students practice finding a specific time period on your classroom time line. The **When in the World Wheel** activity encourages your students to study and create questions about the events pictured in and around each time period on the time line. The ages and skills of your students will determine how in-depth each activity will be. Repeat both activities periodically to have students become familiar with different parts of the time line, react to the new stickers added with each chapter, and to practice and strengthen information-finding skills. Both the cards and wheels can be kept near the lines for children to use to explore on their own.

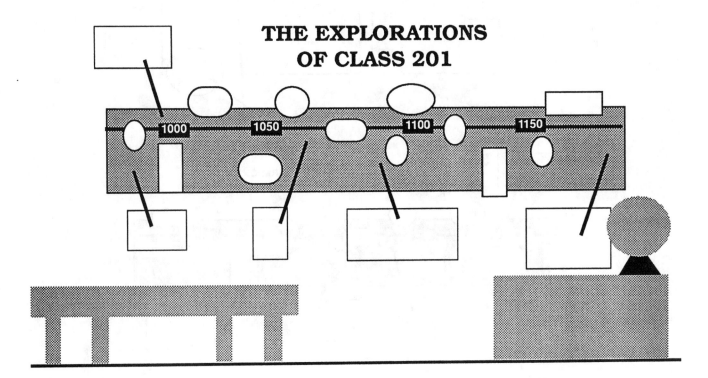

THE EXPLORATIONS
OF CLASS 201

Teacher: Reproduce and assemble the time line prior to starting your explorers activities. Stickers to complete/extend the line further are given in each chapter. Invite your students to include additional dates, pictures and information they discover.

Classroom Time Line Assembly Directions:

1. Reproduce the time line pages and stickers on sturdy paper. Note: you may want to use a different pastel color for each 100-year section.
2. Overlap the time line pages and tape or glue them together. Assemble in one long time line, or two or three smaller sections.
3. Color, cut out, and glue explorers stickers over the gray ovals.
4. More time line stickers are provided in each chapter. Color, cut out, and glue these stickers at the top or bottom of the line as they fit near appropriate dates.
5. Place the time line at child's eye-level on a classroom wall or bulletin board. As your groups do activities or projects related to the events shown, display them above and below the line. Add brightly colored ribbon or yarn to point to the dates or events. Refer to the line often when discussing your topics.
6. Introduce your time line with the Time Travelers and When in the World activities at the end of this chapter.

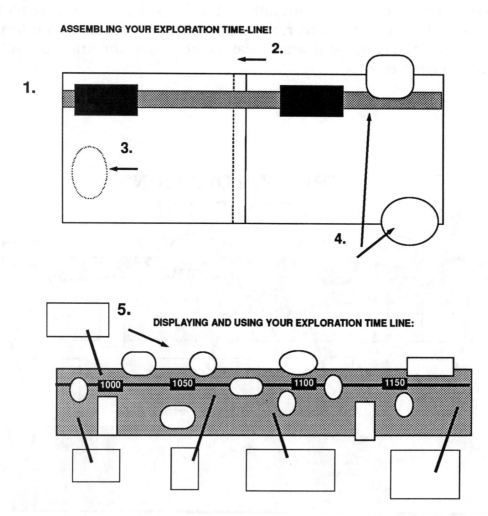

ASSEMBLING YOUR EXPLORATION TIME-LINE!

DISPLAYING AND USING YOUR EXPLORATION TIME LINE:

1000   1050   1100   1150

Classroom Time Line
Reproduce, cut out and assemble.

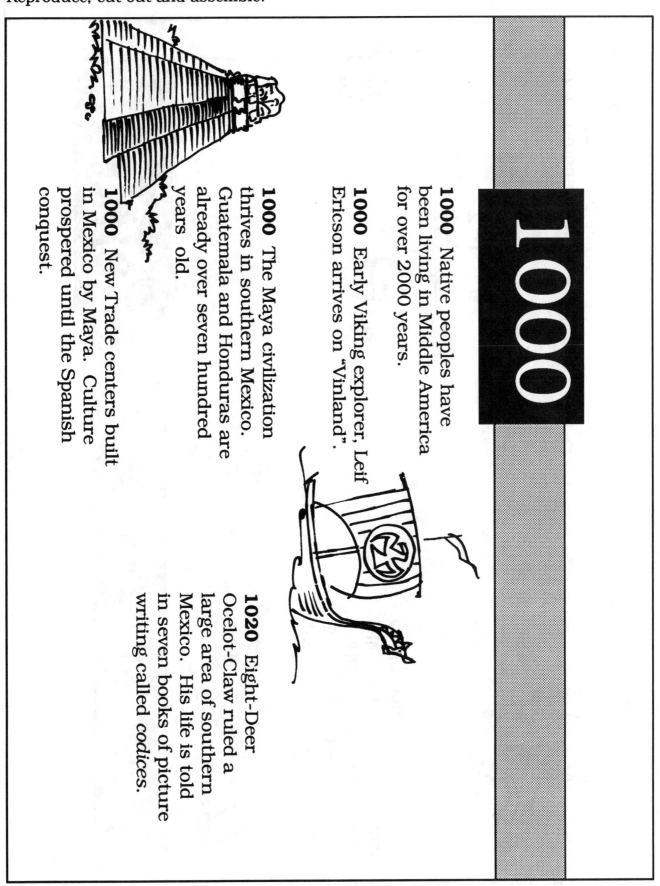

1000 Native peoples have been living in Middle America for over 2000 years.

1000 Early Viking explorer, Leif Ericson arrives on "Vinland".

1000 The Maya civilization thrives in southern Mexico. Guatemala and Honduras are already over seven hundred years old.

1000 New Trade centers built in Mexico by Maya. Culture prospered until the Spanish conquest.

1020 Eight-Deer Ocelot-Claw ruled a large area of southern Mexico. His life is told in seven books of picture writing called codices.

1000

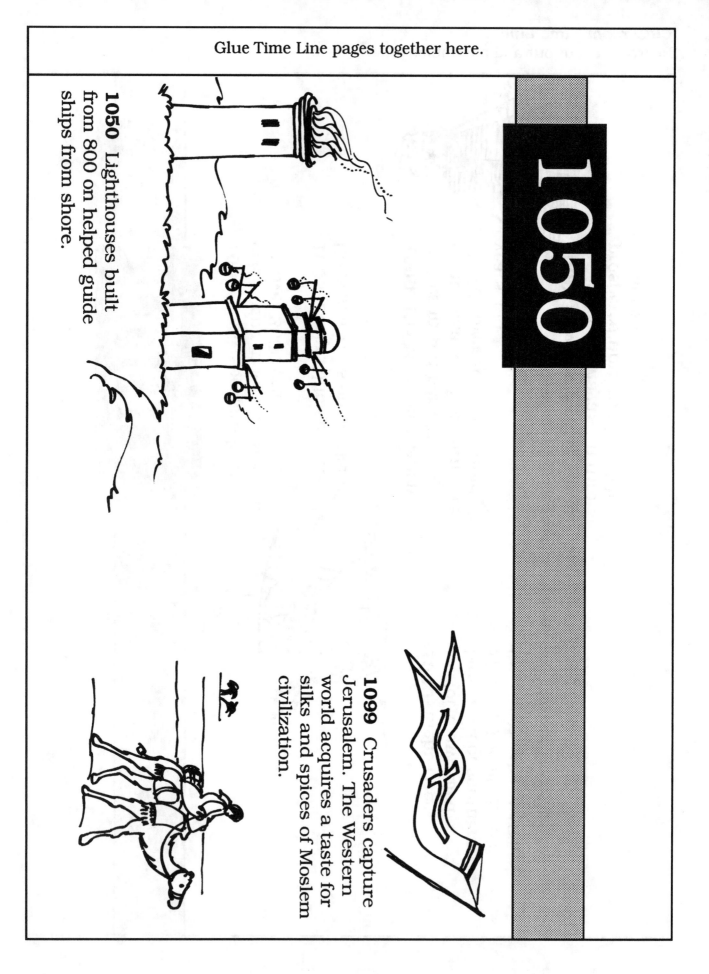

1050 Lighthouses built from 800 on helped guide ships from shore.

1050

1099 Crusaders capture Jerusalem. The Western world acquires a taste for silks and spices of Moslem civilization.

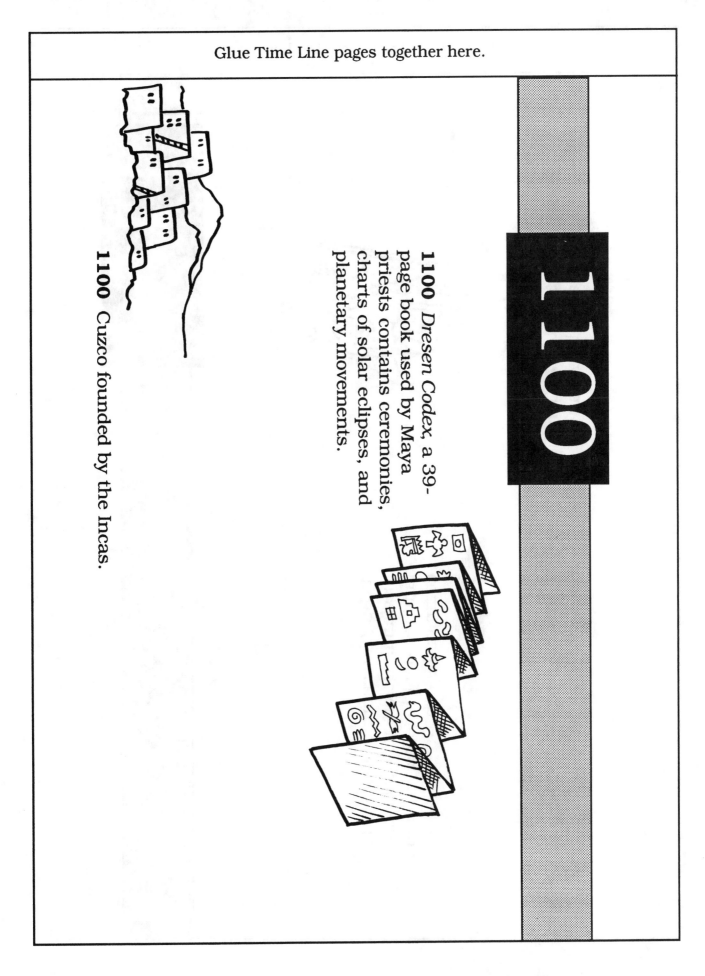

1100 *Dresen Codex,* a 39-page book used by Maya priests contains ceremonies, charts of solar eclipses, and planetary movements.

1100 Cuzco founded by the Incas.

1100

1150

1160 - 1227 Genghis Khan rules Asia.

1185 The chimney is invented in England. Before its development, families slept together around a common hearth.

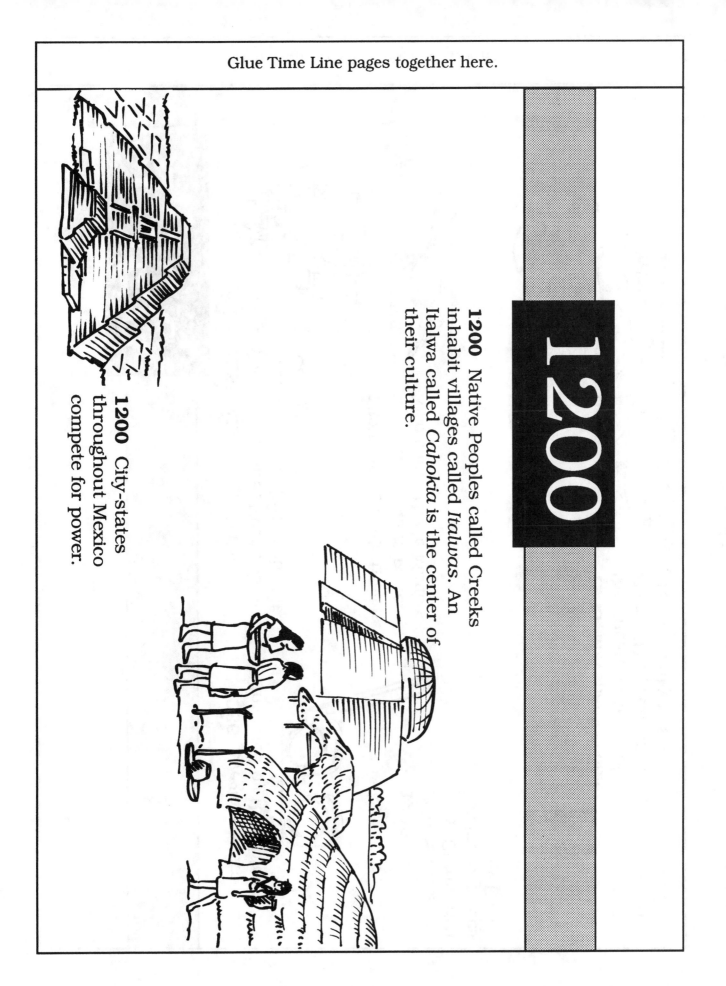

1200

1200 Native Peoples called Creeks inhabit villages called *Italwas*. An Italwa called *Cahokia* is the center of their culture.

1200 City-states throughout Mexico compete for power.

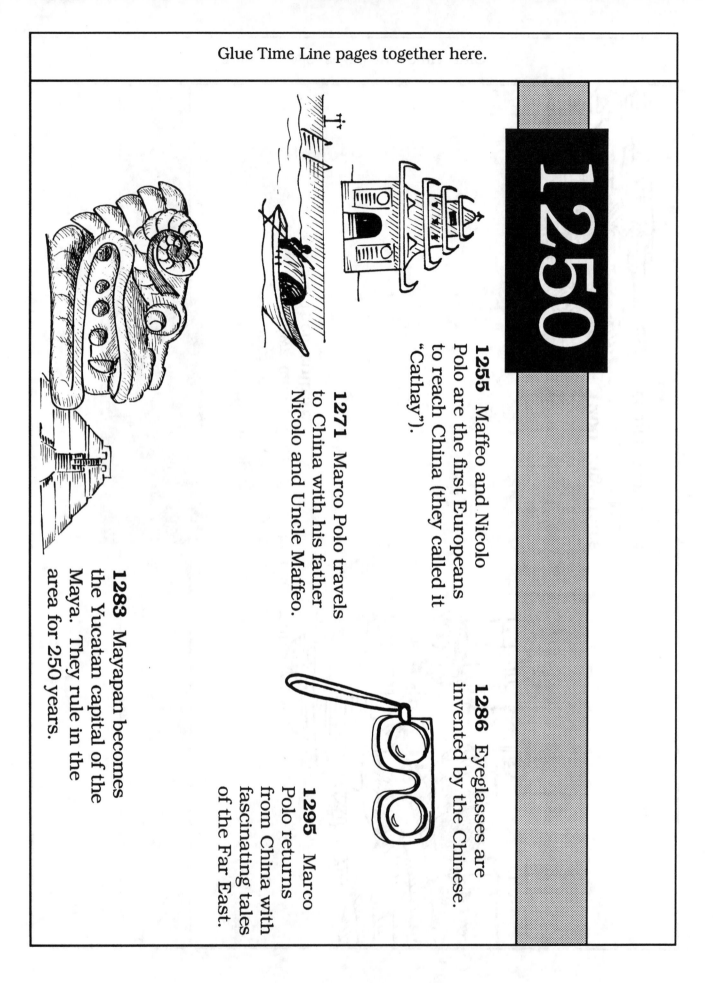

1250

1255 Maffeo and Nicolo Polo are the first Europeans to reach China (they called it "Cathay").

1271 Marco Polo travels to China with his father Nicolo and Uncle Maffeo.

1283 Mayapan becomes the Yucatan capital of the Maya. They rule in the area for 250 years.

1286 Eyeglasses are invented by the Chinese.

1295 Marco Polo returns from China with fascinating tales of the Far East.

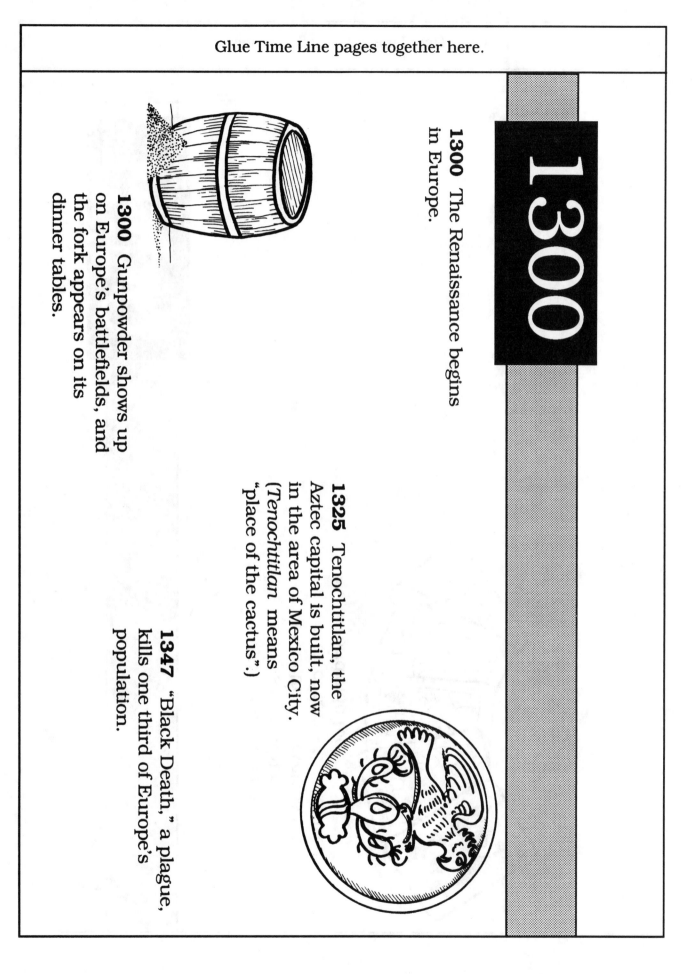

1300

1300 The Renaissance begins in Europe.

1300 Gunpowder shows up on Europe's battlefields, and the fork appears on its dinner tables.

1325 Tenochtitlan, the Aztec capital is built, now in the area of Mexico City. (*Tenochtitlan* means "place of the cactus".)

1347 "Black Death," a plague, kills one third of Europe's population.

1350

1392 Building on a Chinese innovation, a Frenchman develops the deck of cards that is used worldwide today.

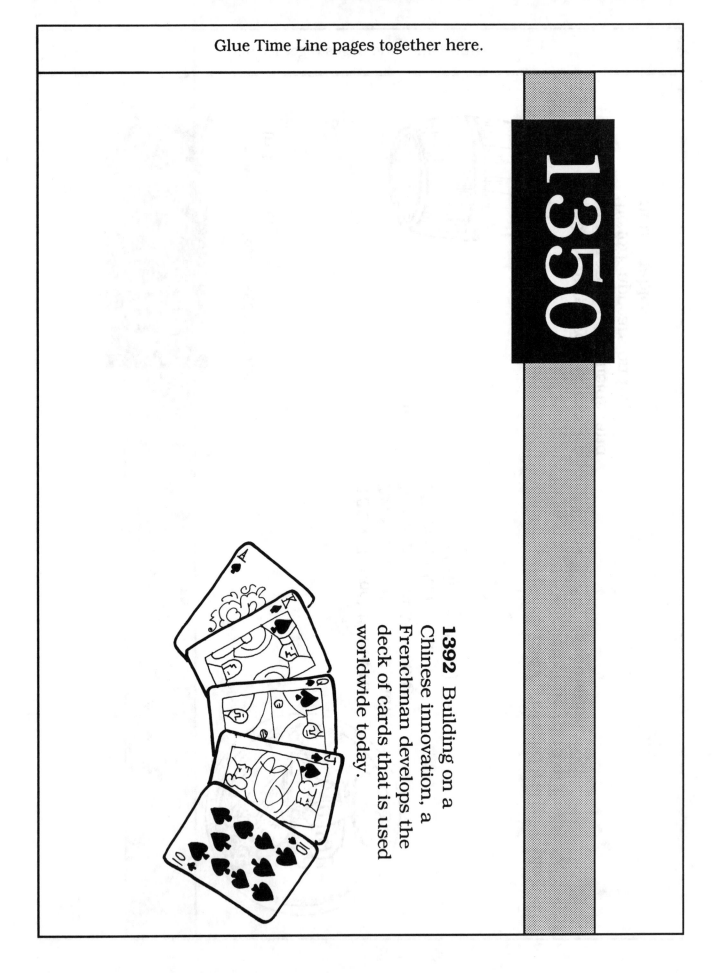

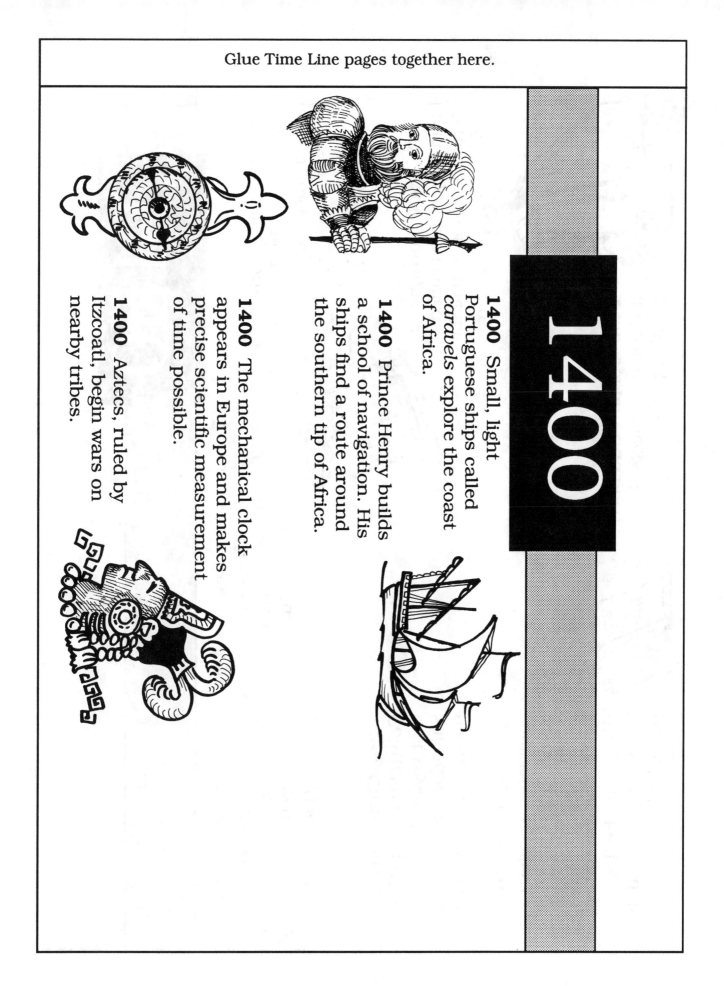

1400 Small, light Portuguese ships called *caravels* explore the coast of Africa.

1400 Prince Henry builds a school of navigation. His ships find a route around the southern tip of Africa.

1400 The mechanical clock appears in Europe and makes precise scientific measurement of time possible.

1400 Aztecs, ruled by Itzcoatl, begin wars on nearby tribes.

1400

1450

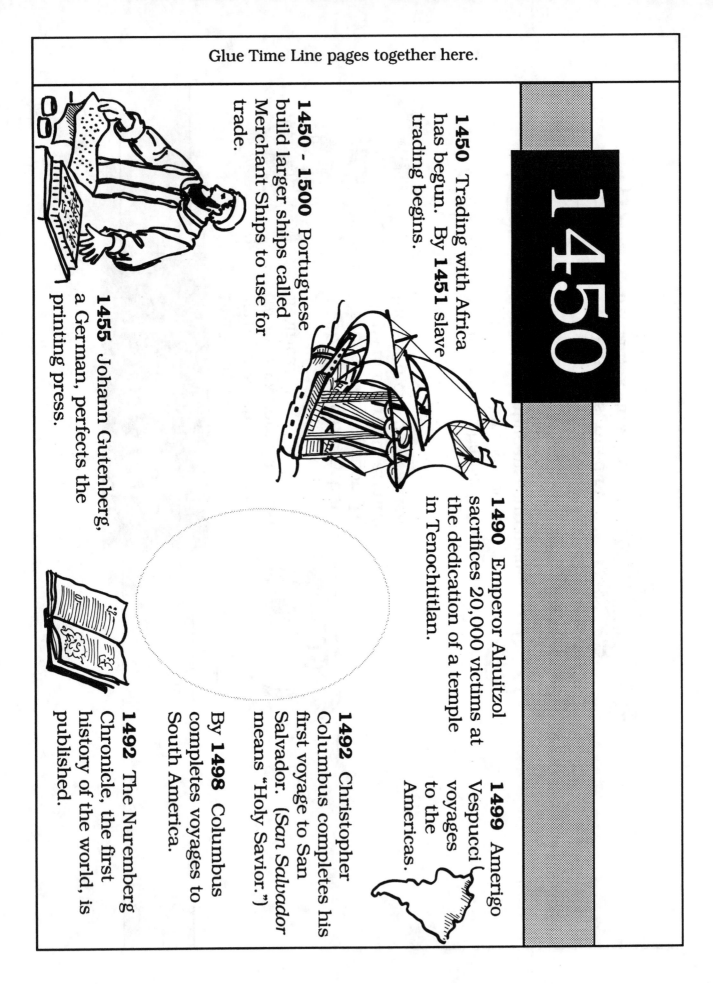

1450 Trading with Africa has begun. By **1451** slave trading begins.

1450 - 1500 Portuguese build larger ships called Merchant Ships to use for trade.

1455 Johann Gutenberg, a German, perfects the printing press.

1490 Emperor Ahuitzol sacrifices 20,000 victims at the dedication of a temple in Tenochtitlan.

1492 Christopher Columbus completes his first voyage to San Salvador. (*San Salvador* means "Holy Savior.")

By **1498** Columbus completes voyages to South America.

1499 Amerigo Vespucci voyages to the Americas.

1492 The Nuremberg Chronicle, the first history of the world, is published.

1500

1502 Montezuma II is the Aztec Ruler.

1506 Christopher Columbus dies believing he'd discovered an unknown part of Asia.

1507 Geographer Waldseemüller names the continent America after mapmaker Amerigo Vespucci.

1518 Spain allows slave-trading.

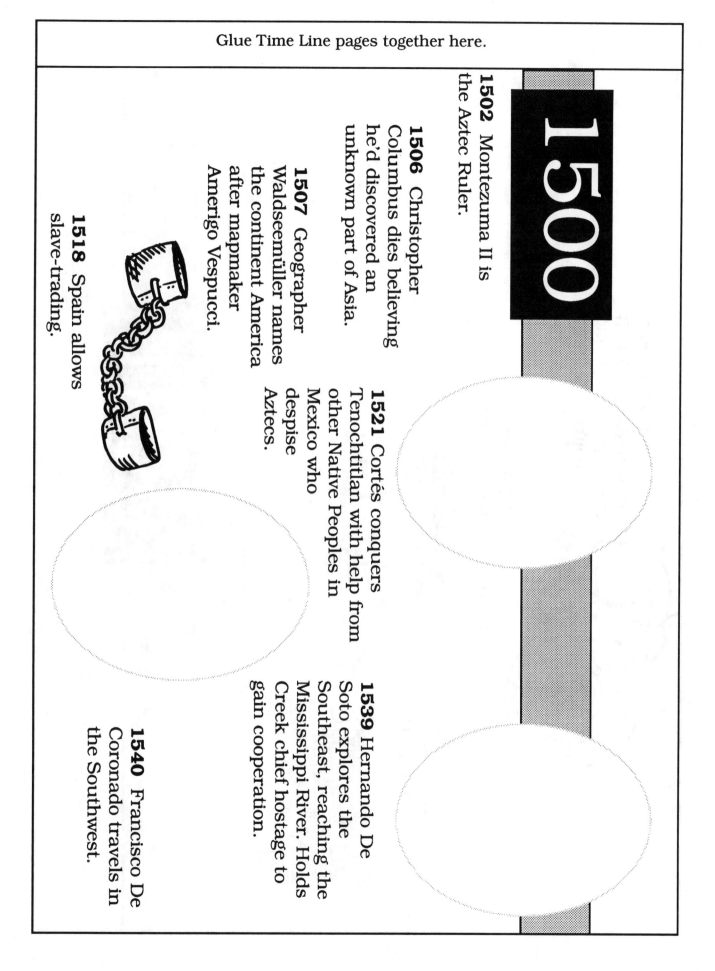

1521 Cortés conquers Tenochtitlan with help from other Native Peoples in Mexico who despise Aztecs.

1539 Hernando De Soto explores the Southeast, reaching the Mississippi River. Holds Creek chief hostage to gain cooperation.

1540 Francisco De Coronado travels in the Southwest.

19

1550

1534 Jacques Cartier is sent by King Francis to find the Northwest Passage.

1550 England builds a speedy fleet of royal ships called Men-of-War.

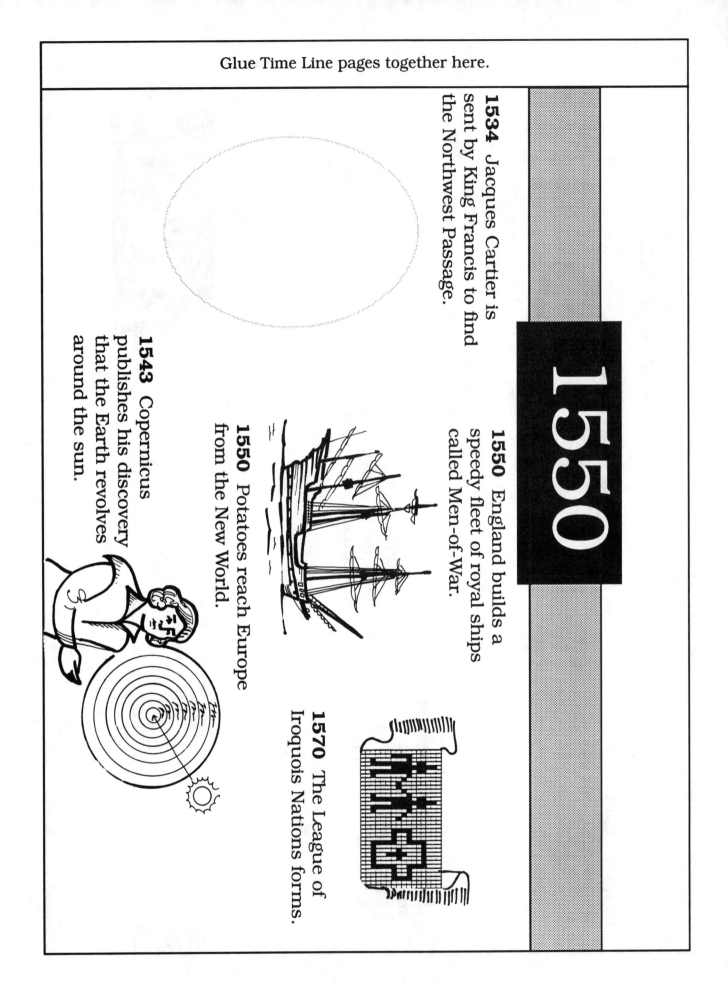

1543 Copernicus publishes his discovery that the Earth revolves around the sun.

1550 Potatoes reach Europe from the New World.

1570 The League of Iroquois Nations forms.

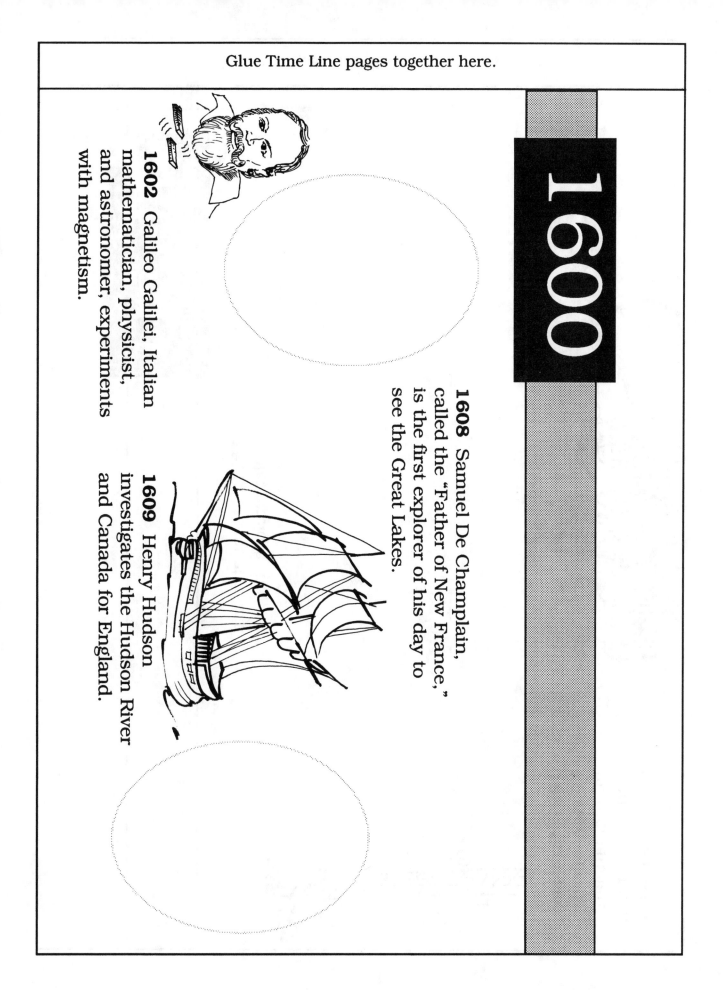

1600

1602 Galileo Galilei, Italian mathematician, physicist, and astronomer, experiments with magnetism.

1608 Samuel De Champlain, called the "Father of New France," is the first explorer of his day to see the Great Lakes.

1609 Henry Hudson investigates the Hudson River and Canada for England.

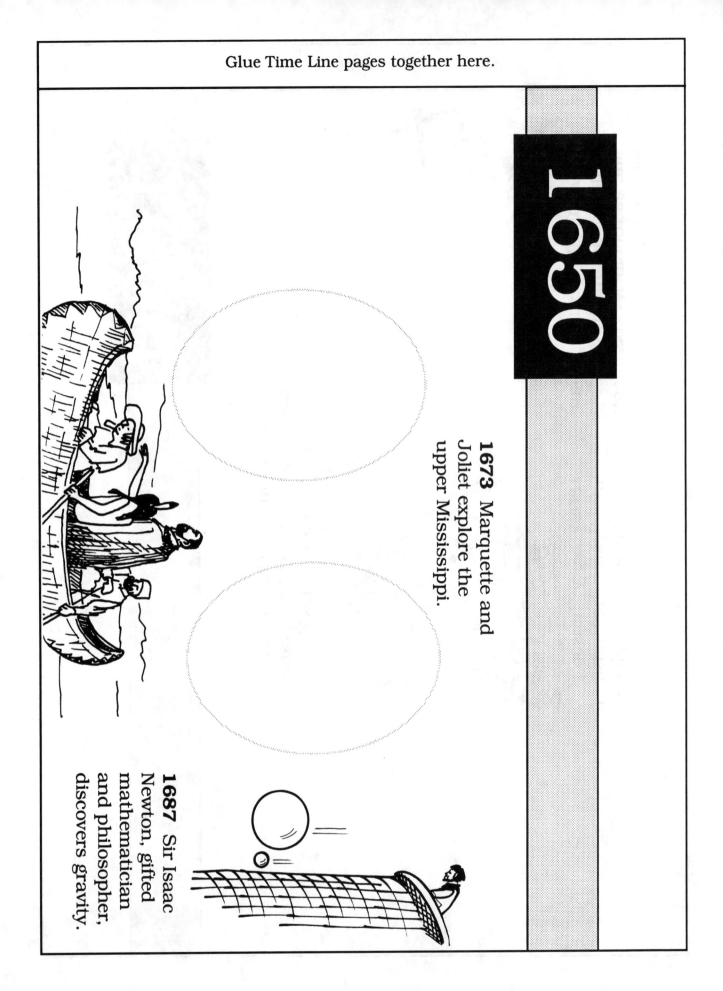

1650

1673 Marquette and Joliet explore the upper Mississippi.

1687 Sir Isaac Newton, gifted mathematician and philosopher, discovers gravity.

Social Skills: Participate, form groups quietly, elaborate.

Academic Skills: Finding a specific time period on a time line.

Teacher: Reproduce 3-4 copies of the Time Travelers cards below so that each student will have one. Pass them out. On your signal, have the students "travel" and line up along the place on the time line that is shown on their card. Follow with the When in the World activity that follows. Note: Keep the cards to switch and use again as you go through the unit.

TIME TRAVELERS

Take a trek along your classroom time line!

When the teacher gives the signal, look carefully at the number on your card. Stand near that number on the time line.

Time Traveler Cards

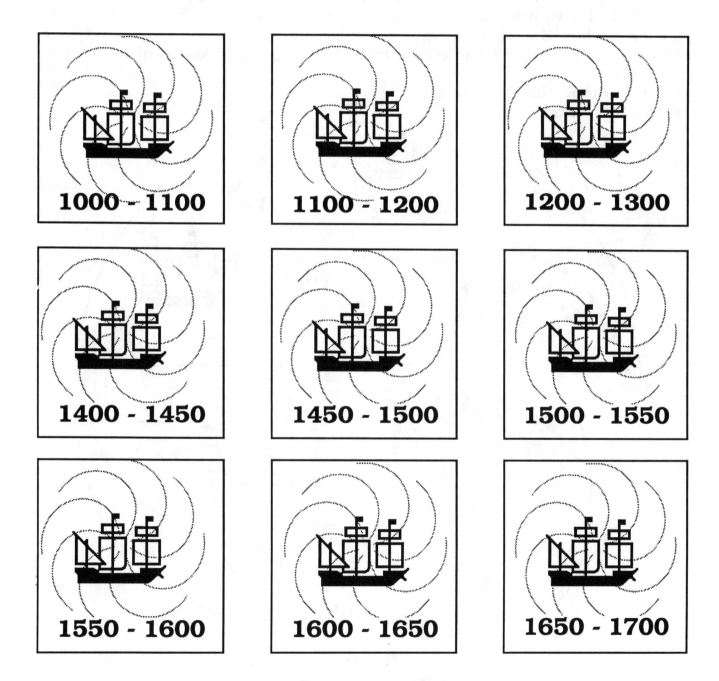

1000 - 1100   1100 - 1200   1200 - 1300

1400 - 1450   1450 - 1500   1500 - 1550

1550 - 1600   1600 - 1650   1650 - 1700

Social Skills: Paraphrase, probe by asking questions, plan out loud.
Academic Skills: Formulating questions from factual dates and events.
Teacher: Reproduce one world wheel top and bottom for each study group. Students from each time period will form study groups near their time line section. Each group will create questions about their time period to finish one wheel. Note: Younger students may need help creating and writing appropriate questions. Display the finished world wheels near the time line for children to use during their free time.

WHEN IN THE WORLD? WHEEL
Create questions to help you explore your time line.

Study Group Directions:
Student 1: Color wheel top.
Student 2: Cut out wheel top and bottom.
Students 1,2,3,4: Write two questions each on the wheel bottom.
Student 3: Punch holes in top and bottom wheel.
Put a brass brad through as shown to assemble.
Students 1,2,3,4: Turn the wheel and answer a question (not your own!).

When in the World?
Wheel Top Pattern

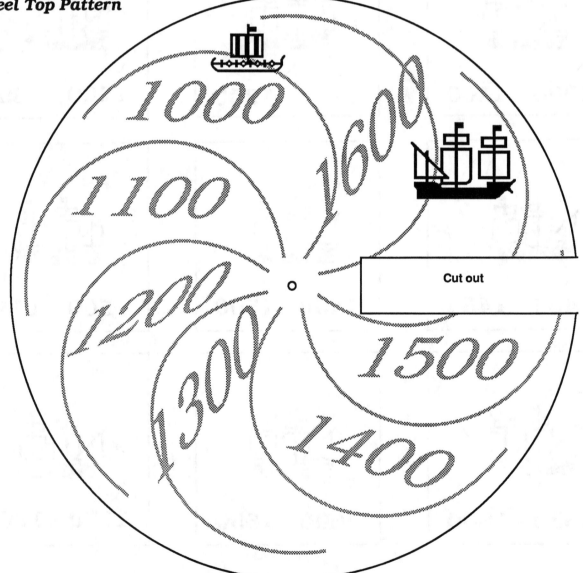

When in the World? Wheel Bottom Pattern
Reproduce this wheel bottom and the top for each study group to use with the When in the World activity.

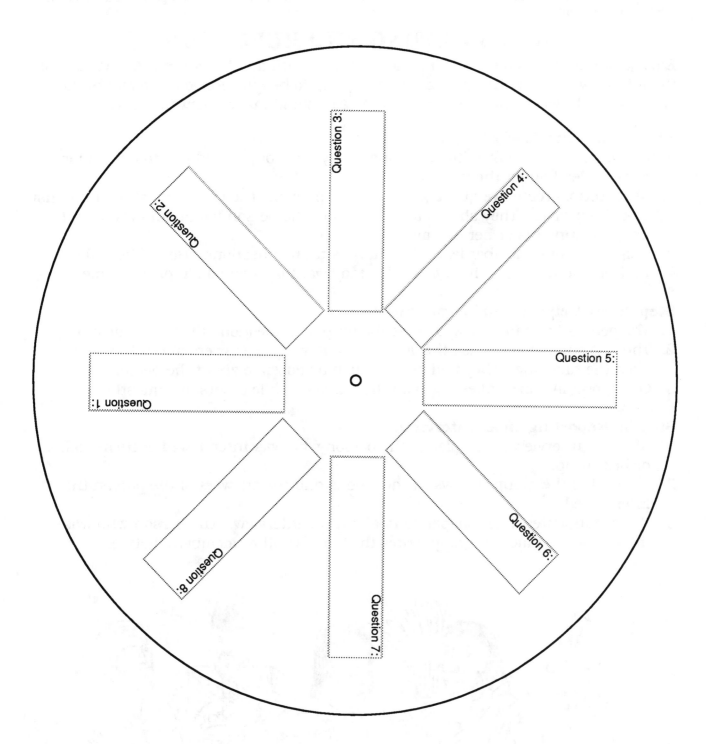

Social Skills: Probe by asking questions, discuss differing opinions quietly and calmly.
Academic Skills: Formulate questions and find answers from various library materials. Report.
Teacher: Reproduce this page for each group. Children can use it for planning and holding interviews throughout the unit. Repeat this activity whenever you want the class to review people and events on the time line.

INTERVIEWING AND REPORTING

Each group prepares one person for an interview with another group. At the time of the interview, that person goes to another group to be questioned. The rest of the group will interview a person from another group and make a newspaper report.

Step 1: Getting Ready for an Interview:
1. Choose one person from the time line that your group would like to know more about. Read about the person.
2. As a group, create five questions about the person. The questions should not just ask about facts. They should ask about how the person felt about events and people during his or her lifetime.
3. Help one group member learn the answers to the questions. He or she will be that person during an interview. You may want to create a simple costume.

Step 2: Participating in an Interview:
1. The person to be interviewed takes the prepared questions to another group.
2. Those group members ask the questions and receive answers about the person from the time line. They find out as much as possible about the person.
3. One group member takes notes on the answers while others ask questions.

Step 3: Reporting on an Interview:
1. After the interview is completed, the person who was interviewed returns to his or her group.
2. The rest of the group reviews the questions and the answers of the person they interviewed.
3. The group writes a newspaper story about the interview. The person who was interviewed by another group writes the story as other members dictate.

Chapter 2
Those Who Dared And What They Dared

European explorers during the Age of Exploration had two main goals. One was to find a shorter, safer route to the Orient and the Spice Islands. The East had treasures and spices and silks that were very popular in Europe. Anyone who found a way to get them quickly and cheaply would gain admiration and riches through their shares in the profits of trade.

The second goal of many explorers was to establish a foothold for their homeland in the New World to reap the wealth and resources they found. Many dreamed of finding gold in fabled ancient cities. Some conquered native peoples and destroyed their cultures. Others lived among the people and traded goods more peacefully.

The explorers began to spread along the shores of the Americas trying to find a way through to the Orient. They searched inlets, bays, and rivers looking for a sea lane. They slowly realized how enormous the barrier was. There were thousands of miles of lands. The search continued for three hundred years. Bit by bit both continents were explored until accurate maps were complete.

The stories behind the explorers' adventures into unknown waters and lands is exciting! We have given you facts and information about several explorers in two forms. **Explorer's Stories** give an account of each man's personal history with information told from his own point of view. **Mini-Books** give short summaries of each explorer's most important voyages or land travels.

These materials are designed to give you basic information to help your students form a clearer picture of each explorer's motivations, his place in history, and to serve as a springboard for gathering more information about each. A limited bibliography of further resources is provided on page 111.

The cooperative activities that follow will work equally well for any other explorers you choose to highlight. Your students' interest and abilities should guide you as to what information will be most meaningful and useful for them.

Explorers Stick-Ons

Reproduce portraits of each explorer on the following pages. Ask groups to color, cut out and add them to the time line.

Note: Make and keep an extra set of these portraits to use on the covers of the **Mini-Books** activity.

Teacher Note: Although much factual information is known about the actual voyages of the explorers, less is known about their personal lives. The following activities are introductions to each explorer. The stories are based on what many historians believe is true about each man. Also in describing the places these men explored, we have often used present-day place names. Be sure the class understands that these places had no European names when they were first seen by the explorers. They are used here to help you track their voyages and land travels on current maps.

Social Skills: Work toward a goal, elaborate, ask for help when needed.
Academic Skills: Create and illustrate a book for any or all of the explorers.
Teacher: Reproduce one Mini-Book Cover (on construction paper), and one Mini-Book page for one explorer (pages 30, 32, 34, 36, 38, 40, 42, 44) on white paper for each group.

MINI-BOOKS
Make history unfold!

Materials: One mini-book cover, one mini-book story, scissors, crayons, tape.

Assembly Directions:

One person completes the cover and puts the book together. The other three group members each illustrate one page of the story.

1. Cut out the cover, glue portrait sticker in place, and fold it along the dotted line.
2. Cut Mini-Book pages apart and pass them out to other group members.
3. Illustrate pages of the story.
4. Pass the book around. Tape each page together in order from 1 to 4, to make one long story strip.
5. Fold the pages like an accordion, back and forth, to fit inside the cover. Pull pages out a bit to stand book up for display.

Assembly Diagrams

This Explorer Mini-Book was made and illustrated by:

_____

_____

_____

_____

Glue the portrait of your explorer here.

Glue the title of your group's book here.

Extending Activity: GIANT BOOK: Ideal for your youngest groups! Choose highlights from the first-person **Explorer Stories** and the **Mini-Books**. Write each idea on a classroom chart or poster board. Pairs draw and color a picture for each. Assemble the charts in order into a classroom "Giant Book of Exploration."

Social Skills: Work quietly, integrate ideas, ask for help when needed.
Academic Skills: Design and illustrate a poster for one or all of the explorers.
Teacher: Enlarge each **Explorer Story** on 11" x 17" tag board. Reproduce any of the tools, glyphs, or other motifs in the book that children may use to decorate the posters.

EXPLORER STORY POSTERS

Europeans and Native Americans had many ways to decorate their books and wall murals. Decide with your partners on a border design for your Explorer Poster and color it. Hang the posters around the classroom or assemble them into a giant classroom book.

Explorer Story

Christopher Columbus
Spain, 1492-1502

I was born Christoforo Columbo in Genoa in 1451. My three younger brothers, one sister, and I grew up in our father's weaving shop. But my dream was always to become a seaman. Every chance I got, I ran down to the docks where ships brought in cargoes of cinnamon and silks from the Indies.

When I was in my teens, my dream came true. I went to sea on the Mediterranean to learn how to do everything on a ship. I learned how to set and weigh (raise) an anchor, how to hand, reef, and steer a ship. I learned how to use navigational equipment like the compass and astrolabe.

Whenever I wasn't working aboard ship, I would work in my brother's map-making business in Lisbon, Portugal. Sailors needed updates of maps as explorers sailed the Atlantic and the coast of Africa. As I studied these maps, I came to wonder if I could sail west to the Indies. I really believed that that would be a shorter and safer route than sailing around Africa to India. I had no money for such a long voyage, so I knew I had to find some rich patron to pay for the ships, crew, and supplies I would need to make the voyage. In May of 1486 I presented my case to Queen Isabella and King Ferdinand of Spain. It took me six years to convince them. On August 3, 1492, I set sail with a crew of ninety men and boys on three ships, the *Niña*, the *Pinta*, and my ship, the *Santa Maria*.

Christopher Columbus
Sailed for Spain: 1492-1502

Mini-Book

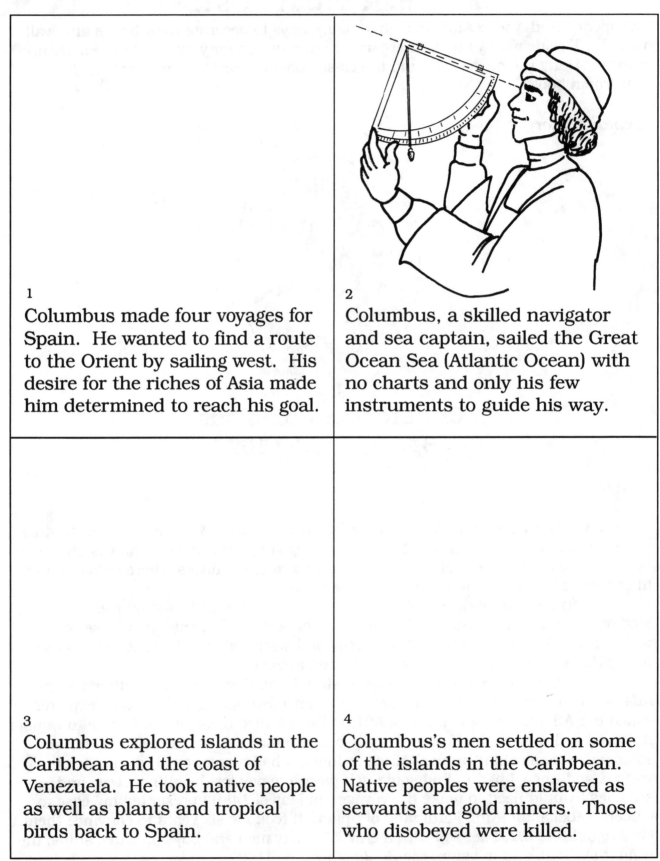

1
Columbus made four voyages for Spain. He wanted to find a route to the Orient by sailing west. His desire for the riches of Asia made him determined to reach his goal.

2
Columbus, a skilled navigator and sea captain, sailed the Great Ocean Sea (Atlantic Ocean) with no charts and only his few instruments to guide his way.

3
Columbus explored islands in the Caribbean and the coast of Venezuela. He took native people as well as plants and tropical birds back to Spain.

4
Columbus's men settled on some of the islands in the Caribbean. Native peoples were enslaved as servants and gold miners. Those who disobeyed were killed.

Hernando Cortés
Spain, 1519-1521

I was seven years old when Columbus made his first voyage across the Atlantic. My father was an army officer in Medellin, Spain. My parents sent me at age fourteen to the University of Salamanca to study law. I learned the basics of law and how to speak and write Latin, the language of learning and diplomacy. I quit school after two years.

I became an excellent horseman and swordsman. I could fire a gun from horseback and hit my target easily. My desire was to be a famous soldier and to get rich in America. In 1504 I got my chance to be a "conquistador" (conqueror). I sailed to Santo Domingo on Hispaniola. The Spanish governor was a friend of the family and I knew he would give me a chance to be a soldier and to find gold. Governor Valasquez finally let me prove myself as a soldier in the conquest of Cuba. He granted me more land in Cuba and more Native American slaves to work it.

When Spanish explorers returned to Cuba from Mexico, the governor learned that the Aztecs there were much richer than the people of Cuba. They had pearls, precious stones, gold, and silver. The governor put me in charge of an expedition to Mexico.

On March 4, 1519 we sailed to the Yucatan Peninsula. After many bloody battles we finally arrived at the capital city of the Aztecs, Tenochtitlan (tay-nahk-tee-tlahn´) where Montezuma II was king. This was the beginning of the conquest of Mexico.

Hernando Cortés
Conquered Mexico for Spain: 1519-1521

Mini-Book

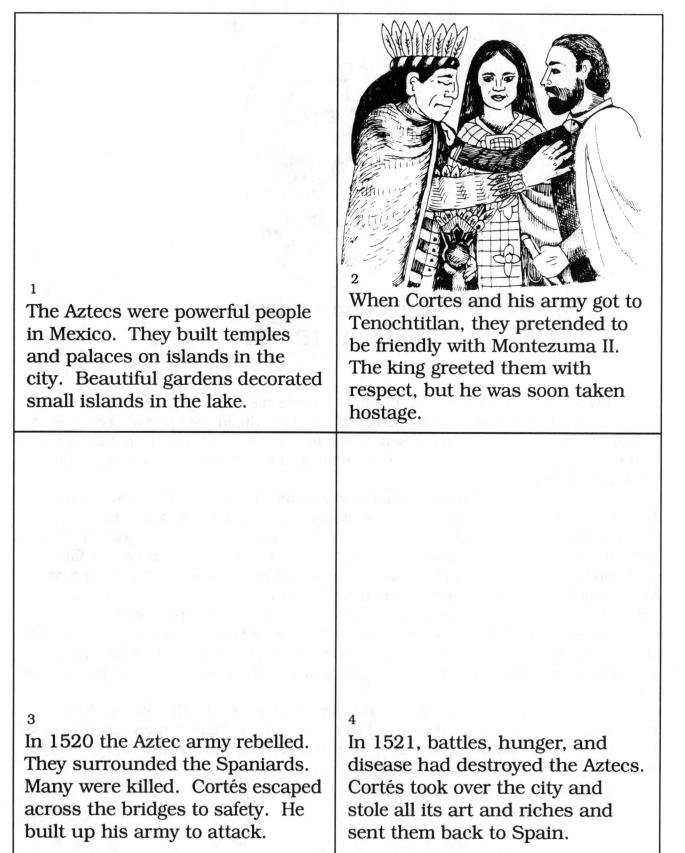

1

The Aztecs were powerful people in Mexico. They built temples and palaces on islands in the city. Beautiful gardens decorated small islands in the lake.

2

When Cortes and his army got to Tenochtitlan, they pretended to be friendly with Montezuma II. The king greeted them with respect, but he was soon taken hostage.

3

In 1520 the Aztec army rebelled. They surrounded the Spaniards. Many were killed. Cortés escaped across the bridges to safety. He built up his army to attack.

4

In 1521, battles, hunger, and disease had destroyed the Aztecs. Cortés took over the city and stole all its art and riches and sent them back to Spain.

Hernando De Soto
Spain, 1539-1542

My father was a poor nobleman. When my parents died, Don Pedrarias adopted me. I grew up in his fine home with the Don's daughter, Doña Isabel. The servants didn't think much of a ragged orphan. On the first day I came to that great house, I was determined to become rich and powerful. Then everyone would have to respect me.

When I was nineteen, Don Pedrarias took me to Panama where he was governor. There I would try to make my fortune and become a hero. Far to the north Cortés had just conquered Mexico. Pedrarias sent me north to conquer Nicaragua with General Cordoba. Later I traveled with Pizarro to Peru where we overran the huge Inca empire of Atahualpa. There I became rich with Inca gold. I returned to Spain and married Doña Isabel.

After so many adventures in Panama and Peru, I grew restless of court life in Spain. The king wanted me to explore Florida in America for him. Peru and Mexico were rich lands: Perhaps Florida was too! The king made me governor of Florida. I was ordered to take an army to explore the area, to make the Indians become Christians, and to start a settlement and hospital.

Isabel and I sailed from Spain with 600 men, 300 horses, and several priests. Isabel stayed in Cuba while my army explored Florida. I was thirty five years old and excited about conquering new lands for Spain.

Note: In 1539 all the lands in the southeast were called "Florida" by the Spaniards. These included Florida, Georgia, North Carolina, South Carolina, Tennessee, Alabama, and Mississippi.

Hernando De Soto
Explored for Spain: 1539-1542

Mini-Book

1

De Soto explored much of the southeast U.S. in search of more gold for Spain. When he found no riches, The native peoples urged him to search further on.

2

The Creeks and other tribes were friendly at first. They allowed the army to visit in their villages. When people were taken prisoner to be carriers, they rebelled.

3

In 1541 De Soto was the first European ever to see the Mississippi River. His men nearly starved and were in rags after travelling for so long in unfamiliar lands.

4

De Soto was weary from the years of protests and battles with many native peoples. He later died of a fever near the Mississippi River in 1542.

Francisco Vásquez de Coronado
Spain, 1540-1542

According to a Portuguese legend from hundreds of years ago, the Moors crossed the Strait of Gibraltar from north Africa and conquered Portugal and Spain. Seven bishops fled Portugal and sailed to a large island in the Atlantic. The island, Antilia, was said to float all around the ocean. The seven bishops each built cities on the island. The cities were very wealthy with magnificent buildings and paved streets. There were gold and jewels everywhere.

I, Coronado, was a Spanish nobleman who lived in Mexico. I worked for Governor Mendoza, the man who ruled the Mexican settlements for our Spanish king. A native slave told the governor that his father traveled north for forty days to the Seven Cities of Cibola. There he found great riches of gold and silver. The buildings had windows and doors framed in turquoise. The slave told the governor that his father came back from Cibola a very rich man. The governor wondered if these seven cities could be the seven cities of Antilia. If he could find them, he would be a famous and rich man. The Spanish had already seized gold and jewels from the Incas in Peru and the Aztecs in Mexico. Here was the chance for more!

So Governor Mendoza sent a Franciscan friar, Fray Marcos de Niza to try to find the cities. He left Culiacán in 1539. He traveled many days across deserts. When the natives told him that they were near the first city, the friar climbed a hill. In the far distance there were many buildings that *looked* like a large city. He wrote back to Mendoza of a handsome city that looked larger than Mexico City. Marcos' story spread through Mexico. We Spaniards were dreaming of gold and glory and so the story appealed to us. The Governor appointed me to head an expedition.

We made a wonderful procession leaving our city. There were over two hundred horsemen wearing shining armor, and silks and velvets of blue, red, and gold. A thousand Indians went along. We took huge herds of cattle and pigs to eat on our long journey to the Seven Cities of Cibola.

Francisco Vasquez de Coronado
Explored for Spain: 1540-1542

Mini-Book

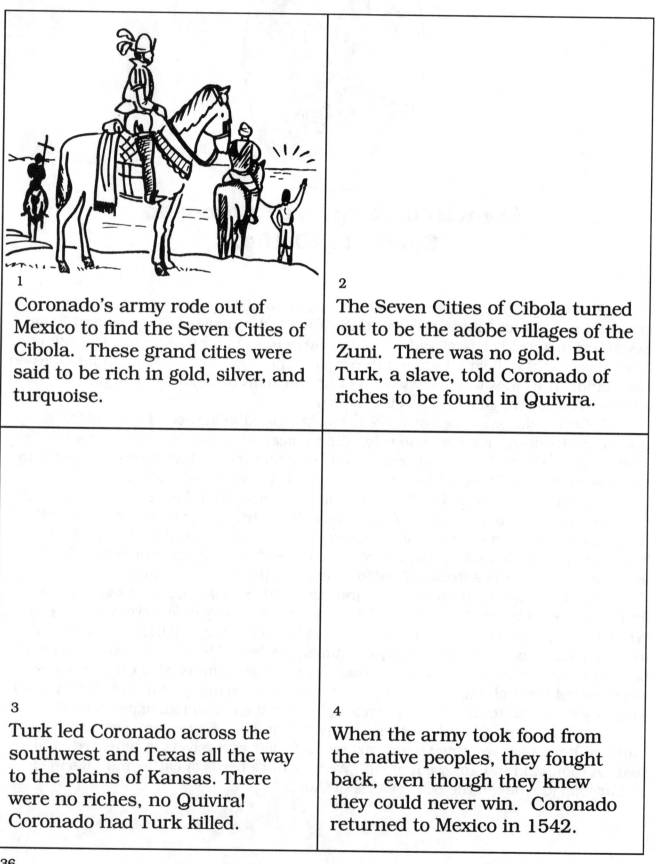

1

Coronado's army rode out of Mexico to find the Seven Cities of Cibola. These grand cities were said to be rich in gold, silver, and turquoise.

2

The Seven Cities of Cibola turned out to be the adobe villages of the Zuni. There was no gold. But Turk, a slave, told Coronado of riches to be found in Quivira.

3

Turk led Coronado across the southwest and Texas all the way to the plains of Kansas. There were no riches, no Quivira! Coronado had Turk killed.

4

When the army took food from the native peoples, they fought back, even though they knew they could never win. Coronado returned to Mexico in 1542.

Jacques Cartier
France, 1535-1543

I was born in 1492, the same year that Christopher Columbus made his first voyage for Spain. Since I was fifteen years old, I had dreamed of exploring the new lands. I had seen the coast of Newfoundland while sailing on my father's ship. None of the other sailors wanted to go ashore to see the island. For years we spent our springs and summers fishing off the Newfoundland coast and our autumns and winters in France.

My reputation as a good sea captain grew. Sailors under my command told others I could find my way through the foggiest seas. Count Brion Chalot was a rich man who played tennis and hunted with the king. He decided to finance my first expedition. He wanted me to find a quicker sea passage between the Atlantic and Pacific to the Spice Islands. He also wanted me to claim lands in North America for France. The area was rich in furs and timber.

Our two little schooners left St. Malo in the spring of 1534. They were small ships, but quick and easy to handle. When we reached Newfoundland, I went ashore for the first time. Sailors shot guillemots, puffins, and auks to eat. One day a birch bark canoe approached our ships. Two young men with shaved heads and waistcloths of marten fur stared up at us. I smiled at them. They came aboard with their canoe. As we sailed down the channel, they tried on our crew's clothes.

We sailed past forests of juniper, pine, beech, and maple. We ate wild red currants, gooseberries, and strawberries. Our new friends took us ashore to meet their chief Donnacona and to feast and dance in their village. They decided to sail back to France with us. They liked France and learned to speak our language. They told us of provinces called Saguenay, Canada, and Hochelaga. We took the men home soon to explore these new areas. They were our interpreters. We did not find a route to the Spice Islands there, but the area was rich for building a new colony. We built a fort and stayed through the winter.

Jaques Cartier
Explored for France: 1535-1543

Mini-Book

1
Cartier left France with three ships in 1535. The two interpreters were happy to sail into Belle Isle Strait past Anticosti Island and up the Hochelaga (St. Lawrence).

2
Cartier was an excellent navigator. High up in the crow's nest, he watched for dangerous waters. He shouted directions to the steersman below.

3
They went up river as far as the Lachine Rapids. After a hard winter Cartier sailed for home. He kidnapped Chief Donnacona and took him back to France.

4
When Cartier returned without the chief in 1541, the village people threatened to attack. Cartier explored the area and sailed back to France in 1542.

Henry Hudson
England and the Netherlands, 1607-1611

I was born in England. My grandfather had sailed with the famous explorer Sebastian Cabot. They started the Muscovy Company to trade with Russia. Three generations of Hudsons had been seafaring men. My son John started sailing with me when he was thirteen. Many trading companies took the long route around Africa to India to buy the spices and other products of the Orient. My company wanted me to find a shorter route north of Europe.

We sailed from England on May 1, 1607. John was one of eleven crew members on board. As we approached Greenland, the weather changed. Strong winds tossed the ship. We had to avoid icebergs that could have wrecked my ship, the *Hopewell*. I decided to change direction. We sailed to a group of islands off Norway where the water was calmer. There were many whales and walruses there. I named the area "Whale's Bay." As we headed back to England, I still had hopes for a shorter route to China, but I knew there was no way for our tiny ship to sail across the frozen North Pole. We sailed back to England for the winter.

John and I studied the charts all during the winter to try to find another route. The Hopewell's hull had to be strengthened against icebergs. The masts were replaced with stronger ones. Arrangements had to be made for stowing more food on board for our longer voyage the following summer.

We left London again on the Hopewell in April, 1608 to sail around the northern tip of Norway. Huge icebergs made sailing the route impossible. I realized we could not sail any further north. I had to admit I could not find a passage northeast around Europe to Asia. We sailed home again to England. The Muscovy Company was not pleased with me. They had paid for two voyages that failed to find a new passage to China. I decided to sail for the Dutch East India Company out of Amsterdam.

Henry Hudson
Explored for England and the Netherlands: 1607-1611

Mini-Book

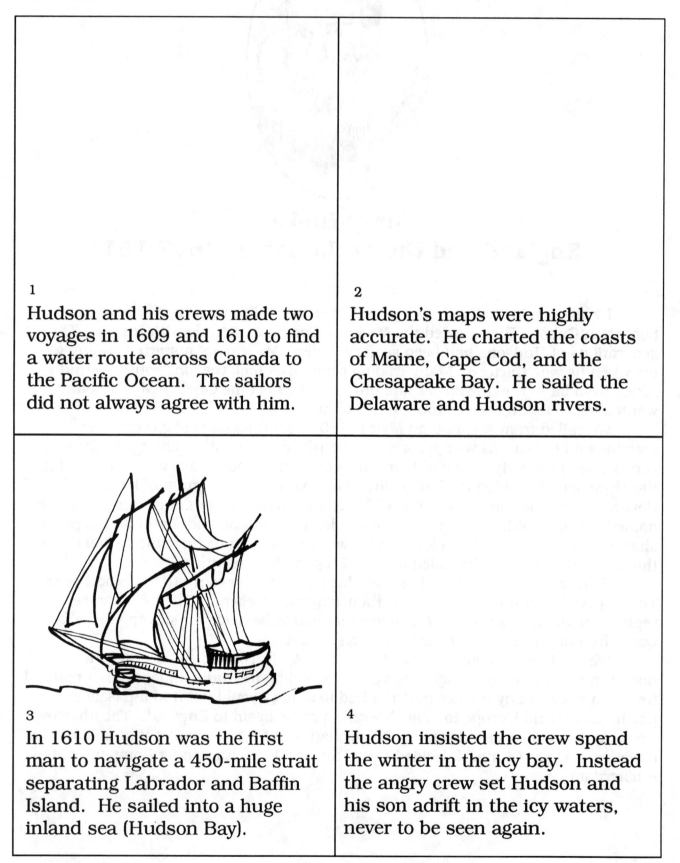

1

Hudson and his crews made two voyages in 1609 and 1610 to find a water route across Canada to the Pacific Ocean. The sailors did not always agree with him.

2

Hudson's maps were highly accurate. He charted the coasts of Maine, Cape Cod, and the Chesapeake Bay. He sailed the Delaware and Hudson rivers.

3

In 1610 Hudson was the first man to navigate a 450-mile strait separating Labrador and Baffin Island. He sailed into a huge inland sea (Hudson Bay).

4

Hudson insisted the crew spend the winter in the icy bay. Instead the angry crew set Hudson and his son adrift in the icy waters, never to be seen again.

Samuel de Champlain
France, 1603-1635

I made my first voyage for King Henry IV of France in 1603. He wanted France to be powerful in the fur trade in America. A colony of fur traders would have to be established. Hats made of beaver fur were very popular with rich Frenchmen. They were handsome hats that lasted a very long time. Beaver was traded with the Native Americans for axes and knives. At the time of our first voyage there were no European settlements in North America north of the Spanish in Florida.

When we reached the St. Lawrence river, we stopped at Tadoussac, then sailed upstream to the Saguenay River. Indians came to trade furs. They said they lived far away by a sea of salt water. So we knew there must be a gulf off the Atlantic. We explored the area for three months. We stopped at Lachine Rapids in the St. Lawrence above Montreal, but our ship and boats were too big to go any further. We traded goods for many furs and sailed home to France.

The King was excited about our discoveries and trade success. I was named the King's Geographer! He sent two ships on our next voyage. For five years we explored the coasts and rivers of North America. I drew maps of the coast. (Note: Champlain charted the coast around the areas that are today called the St. Lawrence, Nova Scotia, and New England areas.)

In 1608 on a jutting headland in the area the natives called Rebec (now Quebec), we started the first large settlement. The Hurons were our neighbors and we traded many furs with them.

Samuel de Champlain
Explored for France: 1603-1635

1

Champlain sailed up the St. Lawrence and Saguenay Rivers as far as Montreal. His mission was to find an area for fur traders to settle and build.

2

Champlain was a good explorer and map maker. He got along well with his Huron neighbors. They traveled by canoe and on foot across a large area.

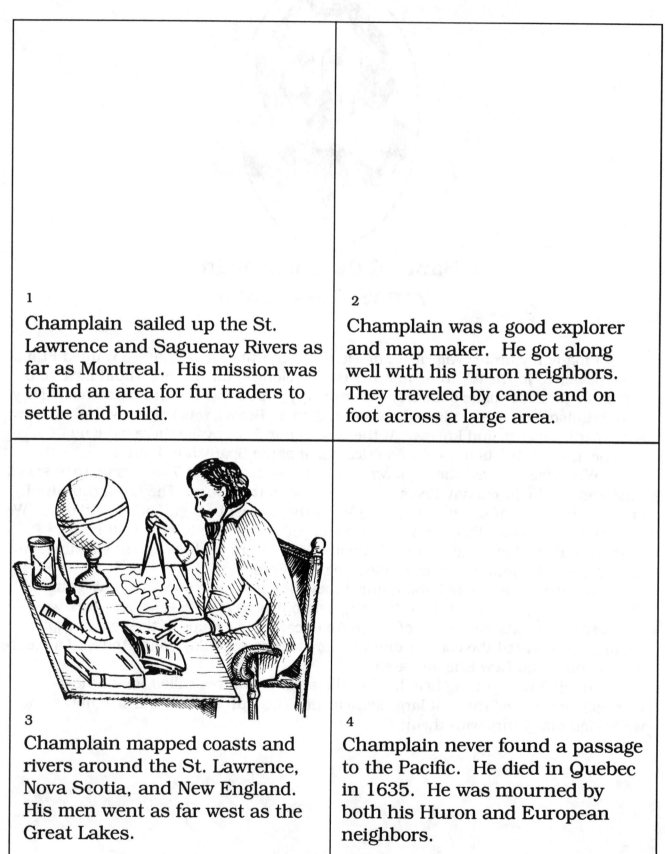

3

Champlain mapped coasts and rivers around the St. Lawrence, Nova Scotia, and New England. His men went as far west as the Great Lakes.

4

Champlain never found a passage to the Pacific. He died in Quebec in 1635. He was mourned by both his Huron and European neighbors.

Father Jacques Marquette and Louis Joliet
France, 1673

I am Father Marquette. I came from France to teach Christianity to the native peoples here in Machilimackinac. My mission was called St. Ignace. When I arrived here I made many friends among the native tribes. I learned to speak to them in their languages. One of my French Canadian friends was Louis Joliet. He was a fine fur trapper and knew the waters around this area very well. Governor Frontenac asked us to find and explore the Mississippi River.

Some of the people here told us of the wide, mighty river called the Father of Waters. They warned us not to go there. They believed in a demon living in the river whose roar could be heard for miles, and who swallowed canoes whole. But Joliet and I did not believe there were demons. We believed this great river might flow west to the Gulf of California and the Pacific Ocean. It could be a passage to the Spice Islands!

There were many people on shore to see us off on our journey. Joliet was waiting for me by our two birch bark canoes. He had a leather pouch with paper, pens, and charcoal which he used to write about and draw what we saw on our journey. Three other Frenchmen made the trip with us. The canoes were loaded with smoked meat, dried corn, muskets, gunpowder, and bullets. Then it was time to find the Mississippi!

Father Jacques Marquette and Louis Joliet
Explored for France: 1673

Mini-Book

1

Marquette and Joliet wanted to find the Mississippi River and explore it. They hoped it ran to the Gulf of California and the Pacific Ocean.

2

They paddled their canoes along Lake Michigan to Green Bay and the Fox River. They had to drag the canoes up rapids and carry them across marshes.

3

Marquette and Joliet finally came to the wild Mississippi. Joliet made notes and drew pictures of all they saw. An Illinois chief gave Marquette a peace pipe.

4

For months they rode downriver. At the Arkansas River Joliet knew that the Mississippi ran to the Gulf of Mexico. The men made the hard trip home to Canada.

Chapter 3
Through Their Eyes—Memoirs of Ancient Peoples

"Spanish civilization crushed the Indian; English civilization scorned and neglected him; French civilization embraced and cherished him."

Francis Parkman
19th-century historian

When European explorers first came to North and South America, they saw at once the abundance of natural resources. However, they did not always see the cultural and intellectual riches of the hundreds of Native American tribes they met here. The Spanish saw the Native Americans as a labor force. The English missionaries wanted to convert them to their own religion of Christianity. The French trappers and fur traders lived among them and traded useful goods for animal pelts. But problems developed when these peoples of different cultures came together. For example, the Europeans did not appreciate or understand the people who lived here; they often tried to change the native peoples' religious beliefs and cultures. They took their riches, their crops, and made many of them their slaves. This chapter looks at some of the culture of these peoples and some of the ways lives were changed during the Age of Exploration.

Time Line Stick-Ons

Symbol of the Aztec City Tenochtitlán

Maya Maize God

Creek Village Scene

Social Skills: Participate, work toward a goal, ask for help when needed.
Academic Skill: Choose a project and follow directions to complete it.
Teacher: Gather all the materials necessary for each of the activities on the following pages. Put each activity in a separate part of the classroom. Children go to an area of interest and work within a group to complete a project. *Rain Player* by David Wisniewski (Clarion Books, 1991)

PEOPLES OF MEXICO—THE MAYA

The Mayas were the first people in the Americas to have a written language. It consisted of picture symbols called "hieroglyphs" (also called glyphs). Hieroglyphs were put in books to record historic events, instructions for planting crops, or how and when to perform ceremonies. They were also carved in stones called "stela". These tall stone statues were carved with an image of a person in the central portion. Hieroglyphic markings on the sides told of events in the person's life. The Mayas also painted beautiful wall murals.

These peace-loving people wore tattoos as symbols of importance. They created elaborate jewelry to wear as bracelets and pendants on the ears, lips, and nostrils. Babies' heads were wrapped to flatten their foreheads, something the Mayas thought of as beautiful. Important people carried feather fans; the bigger the fan, the more important the person was.

Mayas were accomplished scientists. They tracked the planets and knew a lot about astronomy. They developed three types of calendars for agriculture, religion, and one called Long Count that marked all dates.

Religion played a big part in the lives of the Mayas. Rituals and celebrations brought a sense of enjoyment to everyday tasks. There were many gods who were worshipped and who protected the people. The people were reverent toward animals.

Social Skills: Work together. Discuss solutions quietly. Agree on names.
Academic Skill: Create unusual day names from the letters in partners' names.
Teacher: Reproduce the instructions below for each group. Provide drawing paper for glyphs.

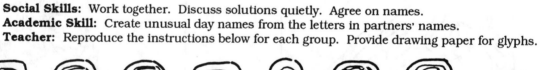

MAYA CALENDAR GLYPHS AND NAMES

On a Maya calendar each day was a *kin*. A month (20 days) was a *uinal*. Each kin had a different glyph, or picture representing it. Some are shown on this page. With your partner write down both of your first names. Make up one kin name for each of seven days using the letters from both your names. Draw a glyph for each kin. Display your kin names and glyphs for the rest of the class to see.

Example: If Phillip and Megan are partners, their kin names might be: hegi, plae, giln, lagi, mehi, lina, and mapi.

Social Skills: Work together. Discuss math problems quietly. Agree.
Academic Skill: Create simple math problems using the Maya numbering system.
Teacher: Reproduce the instructions below for each group.

MAYA MATH

The numbering system used by the Mayas was based on twenty, not ten, like ours. Zero was represented by a sort of shell shaped like a football. Ones were shown as dots; fives, as straight lines. With your partner, make up simple math problems using the number system below. Your answers should not total over twenty. Trade your problems with another group and try to work out your problems together.

Maya Numbering from 0 to 20

0	1	2	3	4	5	6	7	8	9	10

11	12	13	14	15	16	17	18	19	20

Example: *(3 + 5 = 8)*   ••• + ——— = •••

Your Math Problems:

Extending Activity: Use other geometric symbols or glyphs to make up your own numbering system.

Social Skills: Discuss solutions, seek accuracy, extend another's answers.
Academic Skill: Design a game and write the rules for playing it.
Teacher: Reproduce the chart below for each group.

RAIN PLAYER

Read the wonderful book *Rain Player* by David Wisniewski in your group. Pik is a Maya *pok-a-tok* game player who challenges Chac to bring rain to his people. Work on an activity to tell about the book or work together to complete one of the projects.

Make a Pok-a-Tok Game

> **"He blocked a pass with his shoulder and sent the ball flying
> through the stone ring above his head."** from *Rain Player*

Discuss in group how the game would be played as it was shown and described in the story. The game is sort of a combination of basketball and soccer. A rubber ball was used to make "baskets" and hands could **not** be used to make a goal. Write the rules of the game below. Try playing your game together.

Pok-a-Tok	
Equipment:	**Object of the Game:**
	How to Play the Game:
Team (number of players, positions of players, etc.)	**Scoring the Game:**
	Ending the Game:

48

Social Skills: Work toward a goal, ask for help when needed.
Academic Skill: Follow directions carefully to make a headdress.
Teacher: Gather all the materials listed. Reproduce one page for each group of four.

MAYA HEADDRESS

Colorful tropical birds lived in the forests where Pik lived. Their feathers were used to make beautiful headdresses and to decorate clothing. The cut-paper art in *Rain Player* helped make the story exciting to read. Your group can make a version of the headdress Pik wore in the pok-a-tok game against Chak.

Materials:
24" piece of wide elastic per group
Green, red, and orange paper
Tissue paper in 2 shades of blue
Tacky glue
Scissors
Patterns on this page

Assembly Diagrams

tie

To Make:
1. Trace 5 of each pattern on green, orange, and red paper. Cut them out.
2. Cut six 6" x 2 1/2" "feathers" of both shades of blue tissue paper. Fringe edges.
3. Cut six 18" x 3" "feathers" of both shades of blue tissue paper. Fringe the edges.
4. Lay the elastic flat on the table. Glue the leaves to the back of the elastic. Place first leaf in center; then add two more on each side. Leaves can overlap. Allow to set.
5. Glue the large flowers to the elastic in front of the leaves. Allow to set.
6. Glue the small flowers on top of the large ones. Allow to set.
7. Turn the band over. Glue the 6" feathers behind the leaves in the center of the band. Allow to set.
8. Glue the 18" feathers behind the leaves on the left and right sides of the elastic Allow to dry throughly before trying on.
9. To wear, tie ends of elastic at the back of your head.

small flower
(orange paper)

large flower
(red paper)

leaves
(green paper) 49

PEOPLES OF MEXICO—THE AZTECS

According to an ancient legend, the Aztecs believed they should make a settlement when they saw a sacred "sign": A live eagle holding a serpent in its claw would be perched on a cactus that grew from a rock. This location was in the middle of a swamp surrounded by lakes. The Aztecs a built beautiful city of polished stone, silver, and other riches using their cleverness and ingenuity. Their gardens were made on rafts piled with dirt. They floated in the lakes around the city. Eventually the roots from the plants reached the bottom of the lake and secured the rafts in place permanently.

The Aztecs were warlike people. Warriors, highly respected, wore armor engraved with serpents, jaguars, and tigers. They captured people from other tribes and enslaved them or sacrificed them at their magnificent temples.

They created a stone-wheel calendar and could predict changes and events by studying the stars. The Aztecs wove fine cotton cloth trimmed with feathers and animal fur. Their elaborate jewelry was created with gold, silver, jade, turquoise, and semi-precious stones. Like the Mayas, the Aztecs used glyphs to communicate.

Example: Montezuma traveling out of Tenochtitlán to the house of the ocelot.

Aztec Glyphs
Use with the Story Mural on page 51.

traveling

stone

Montezuma

tree

Tenochtitlán

teeth

Social Skills: Participate, extend another's ideas, agree on answers.
Academic Skill: Create an animal story using glyphs.
Teacher: Reproduce this page and page 49 for each group.

AZTEC GLYPH STORY MURAL

Painted murals decorated walls of palaces and temples. Many told stories of animals or of great events in Aztec history.

Materials:
24" sheet of freezer paper
Glyphs
Markers
Scissors

To Make: Work together to write an animal story using the glyphs below or others of your own design. Each person colors several glyphs. Then take turns gluing them in place on the freezer paper to make a mural to hang near the time line.

Aztec Glyphs

lizard

crocodile

wind

house

rabbit

water

Death's head

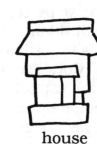

deer

reed

ocelot

monkey

grass

knife

rain

vulture

motion

eagle

flower

serpent

dog

51

Doña Marina

I am Malintzin, the daughter of a Tobascan chieftain. When Cortés came to Mexico in 1519, he gave me the Spanish name Doña Marina. I became his interpreter. As we traveled toward the Aztec capital, Cortés learned from me about Montezuma. He was the emperor of all the Aztecs, the richest and most feared man in Mexico. For 150 years, Aztec armies had conquered many of the other warriors in the Valley of Mexico. Prisoners were sacrificed on the steps of great stone temples of the capital city, Tenochititlán. The survivors of these towns were ready to help Cortés in his battle against the Aztec armies.

Cortés and his mighty army of conquistadors and native warriors marched into the capital city. They held Montezuma hostage for all the gold and other riches his empire possessed. Cortés later returned to Spain in glory, with more riches than he had ever dreamed of.

Emperor Montezuma II

I was the leader of all the Aztecs. In the months before Cortés came to Tenochtitlán my servants told me of his arrival in Mexico. At first I mistook the Spaniard for *Quetzalcoatl* (kweh´-tsal-koh-wah´-til), an ancient Aztec god who had been banished by my ancestors. Legends said that Quetzalcoatl was a tall, fair-skinned man with a beard. He had promised to come back to the Valley of Mexico to punish the Aztecs for sending him away. The Aztec calendar showed that Quetzalcoatl would return in the year *ce acatl*. 1519 was the year of ce acatl. I was sure that Cortés was the angry god. So I sent two ambassadors to him with lavish presents of gold and white cloth trimmed in gold feathers. Perhaps Cortés could be bribed into leaving my empire in peace.

On the day that this "god" rode into our capital city with his armies, we greeted him in a friendly way. Cortés gave me presents of beads and a red cap. But he took me prisoner and forced me to give him larges amounts of gold! Thousands of Aztecs were killed in battles. Thousands more died of smallpox, a terrible disease brought by the Spaniards. The Aztec empire, built over hundreds of years, was destroyed forever.

52

Social Skills: Work quietly, extend another's answers, agree on answers.
Academic Skill: Express several different persons' points of view of the same scene.
Teacher: Reproduce the Picture Cards below and Story Cards on page 52 for each group. Give each group a large sheet of drawing paper.

DIFFERING POINTS OF VIEW

Not everyone feels the same way about the same event. The Picture Cards below have pictures of Cortés, Doña Marina, and Montezuma. Read the Story Cards and other materials about these people. With your partner, decide what each person is thinking. Cut the cards apart. Paste the cards on a large piece of drawing paper. Write what they are thinking above them in balloons, as in a comic book.

Picture Cards

PEOPLES OF AMERICA—THE CREEKS

The Creeks lived in what is now the southeast United States. Their communities were made up of large farming chiefdoms. Each one had its own ruler, the chief, who ruled over all the people. Their towns, called *Italwas*, were built around a large area with a council house, a town square and a game field. In this area all their ceremonies were held.

They grew corn, beans, and squash, as well as cotton. Women tended the fields while men hunted and fished. Religion was part of daily life. The people had a reverence for nature and the earth. Their art showed this reverence with patterns of flowers and animals. They carved and engraved stone and shell necklaces, and made stone statues and weapons. These people did not have a written language. They communicated orally. When Europeans came, they brought war as well as diseases with them. Many Creeks lost their lives. Much of their oral history and many of their traditions died with them.

Social Skills: Participate, extend another's ideas, agree on answers.
Academic Skill: Work together to create a celebration.
Teacher: Help children research costumes and Native American dances and instruments.

GREEN CORN CELEBRATION

Each year when the corn was ready to be harvested, the Creeks held the Green Corn Ceremony. They feasted and danced and gave thanks for the successful crop of corn. The old Council Fire was put out and a new one was lit, symbolizing a new season and a new year. What other way way might **you** celebrate a "new beginning" (start of school year, return after winter break, the start of summer vacation, etc.)? Plan a celebration in your group and prepare materials for costumes, feasting, or dancing. Share your festivities with the class.

Social Skills: Participate, extend another's ideas, agree on answers.
Academic Skill: Follow directions to create a beaded craft.
Teacher: Reproduce the directions below for each group. Copy some of the spices and plants illustrated in Chapter 5 for groups to use as patterns.

CREEK BEADING

Creek women often created beaded pouches and clothing using patterns from nature such as flowers, plants, or animals. You can make a "beaded" pouch with dried, colored rice.

Materials:

Uncooked rice
Food coloring in various colors
Boiling water
White vinegar
Plastic spooons
Small coated paper bowls
Paper towels
Plastic sandwich bags
Tacky glue
Plain envelopes

To Dye Rice:

Each person in the group dyes one batch of rice. You may want to dye the rice at home and bring it to school to share with the group. Make sure each person uses a different color.

1. Pour 1/2 cup boiling water into a bowl.
2. Add 1 teaspoon white vinegar.
3. Add food coloring drop by drop until you get the shade you want.
4. Stir in 1/3 cup rice.
5. Spoon rice onto paper towels. Allow to dry.
6. Put each batch of colored rice in a plastic bag.

To Make a Beaded Pouch:

1. Place bags of colored rice where everyone in the group can use them for their own design.
3. Each person draws a flower or plant design on an envelope.
4. Spread a small amount of glue in a small area of the design.
5. Cover the area with the desired color of rice. Continue gluing rice to small areas a little at a time until the design is completed.
6. Allow to dry. Use your pouch to store co-op cards from other activities.

Chapter 4: Tools of Discovery

"The art of navigation demonstrateth how by the shortest good way, by the aptest direction, and in the shortest time, a sufficient ship...be conducted."
Dr. John Dee, English scholar and teacher of navigation, 1550

Navigating a vessel took great skill and courage, and much experience. Mariners made use of every one of their senses. They **watched** coastlines for landmarks, capes, lighthouses, beacons or buoys that could give them clues about the places they were sailing to. They checked the waters carefully; noticing the color and the clarity of the seas around them. Log lines were dropped with wax plugs in the bottom to gather samples from the ocean floor to see what the sea bottom looked like beneath them. Navigators looked up into the skies and out at the horizons at sea both day and night. Almanacs, maps, charts, tables and logs were studied as sailors searched for information to make their journey safer or shorter.

Mariners **listened** for the Captain's orders, the piping of the Boatswain's (bosun's) signals and the toll of the bell signaling watch. The sounds of the rushing tides, birds that signaled land was near, and storms that were brewing on the seas were all familiar to experienced ears. Even the winds had distinctive sounds!

The sailors' sense of **smell** alerted them to fires on their wooden vessels during storms; or to rotting fish in the hold below, or to the smells of trade winds that could blow up and help or hinder them.

The expert **touch** of ship builders made faster, easier-to-handle ships. "All hands on deck" describes the ship's crew whose hands were never idle! Pilots brought the ships into harbor. The boatswain handled all the cords, ropes and sails. The ship surgeon served as the doctor. "Coopers" repaired all the buckets and barrels on the ship--that meant enough food and water in the ship's hold! Other jobs, such as the master gunner, carpenter, and cook, were important, too. "Yonkers" (15-20 year old men) and "grummets", (young cabin boys) were learning their trade to keep each ship sailing on course. Astronomers, mathematicians and geographers aided captains by creating more accurate tools to tell wind and course direction, speed of ship, longitude, and latitude.

Navigating also was very detailed work. Besides being constantly aware of every sight and sound, the crew recorded all observations on slates, charts, in logs and as journals. Every aspect of each trip was charted and noted, hourly and daily. It was the accumulation of this information over more than 200 years that made better trade routes and safer navigation possible. Bit by bit, these energetic adventurers were defining and encountering the new world...down coastlines, along continents – out ever farther into the unknown.

EXPLORER'S TOOLS STICK-ONS

1492 Martin Behaim makes the first world globe in Germany.

1380 Navigators are now skilled at using the compass.

1650 Cartographers make sea charts and globes to help explorers.

1540 Sailing manuals are published in Portugal.

1609 Galileo constructs the first telescope to observe the moon.

1550 Sea charts printed in the Netherlands are readily available.

1000 Early Egyptian explorers used lead-lines with wax-filled lead weights to measure water depth.

1550 Log and log lines were used to check a ship's speed every hour.

1490 Cross-staff used to measure the altitude of a heavenly body and compare it with position of the ship.

Boatswain's Pipe

Sliding Scale

Social Skills: Jog memory of teammates, participate, work toward a goal.
Academic Skills: Match pictures and definitions of navigational tools.
Teacher: Make a set of Cabin Sheets (pages 59-62) and Stick-ons (pages 57 and 58) for each group. The assembled cabin page will be passed around, having members match and glue stickers. Note: There are extra stickers for students to place anywhere they choose.

CAPTAIN'S CABIN STICK-ONS

Each group member: Cut out a set of tools stickers. Then pass the cabin sheets around the group and take turns placing a sticker on the right outline.

Explorer's Tools Stick-ons

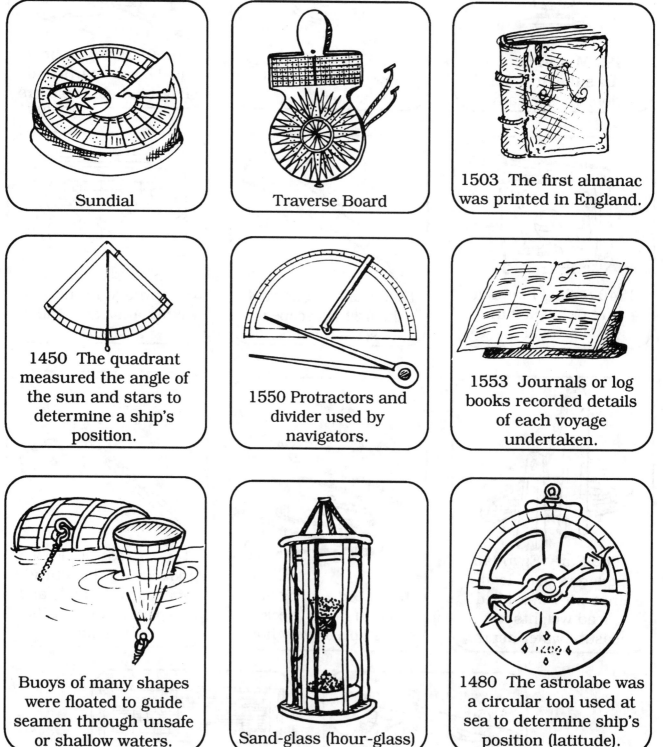

Sundial

Traverse Board

1503 The first almanac was printed in England.

1450 The quadrant measured the angle of the sun and stars to determine a ship's position.

1550 Protractors and divider used by navigators.

1553 Journals or log books recorded details of each voyage undertaken.

Buoys of many shapes were floated to guide seamen through unsafe or shallow waters.

Sand-glass (hour-glass)

1480 The astrolabe was a circular tool used at sea to determine ship's position (latitude).

Captain's Cabin Sheet Piece A:

To assemble, overlap and glue A to B where shown. Use with the Explorer's Tools stick-ons on page 57 and 58.

Sand-glasses (hour-glasses) used on ship kept track of the time and speed of the ship. There were different sizes: watch-glass (four hours), half-watch (2 hours), or minute glass.

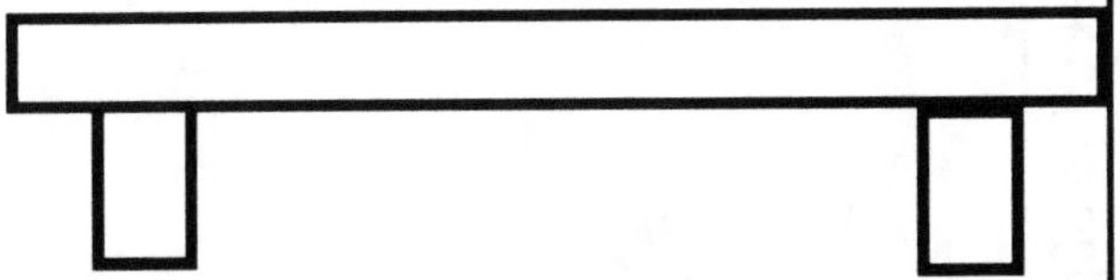

Mariners used sun dials along with sand-glasses to tell the time while on ship.

The quadrant was a tool used to measure the angle of the sun and stars to determine a ship's position.

Journals or log books were used to record information such as: date, true course, leagues sailed (distance), winds, latitude, longitude, variations off course and other remarks.

Captain's Cabin Sheet Piece B.

Glue to piece A. Use with the Explorer's Tools stick-ons on pages 57 and 58.

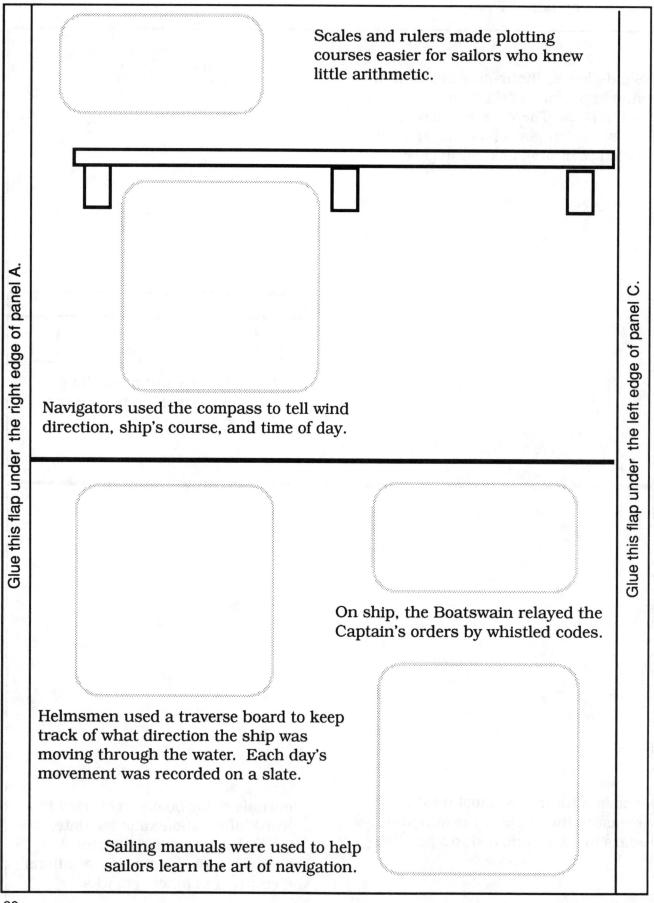

Scales and rulers made plotting courses easier for sailors who knew little arithmetic.

Glue this flap under the right edge of panel A.

Glue this flap under the left edge of panel C.

Navigators used the compass to tell wind direction, ship's course, and time of day.

On ship, the Boatswain relayed the Captain's orders by whistled codes.

Helmsmen used a traverse board to keep track of what direction the ship was moving through the water. Each day's movement was recorded on a slate.

Sailing manuals were used to help sailors learn the art of navigation.

Captain's Cabin Sheet Piece C.

Glue to piece B. Use with the Explorer's Tools stick-ons on page 57 and 58.

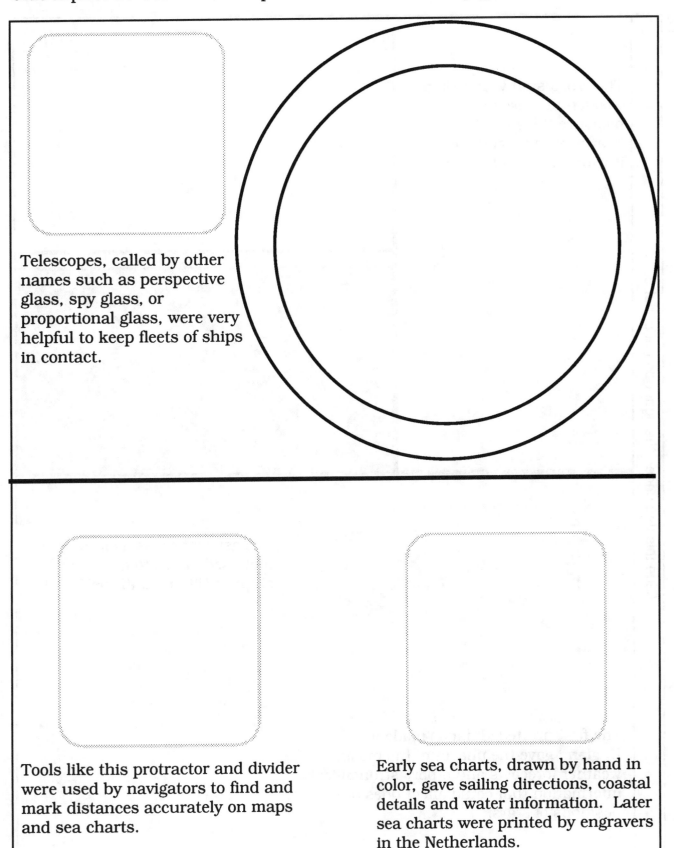

Telescopes, called by other names such as perspective glass, spy glass, or proportional glass, were very helpful to keep fleets of ships in contact.

Tools like this protractor and divider were used by navigators to find and mark distances accurately on maps and sea charts.

Early sea charts, drawn by hand in color, gave sailing directions, coastal details and water information. Later sea charts were printed by engravers in the Netherlands.

Captain's Cabin Sheet Piece D.

Glue to piece C. Use with the Explorer's Tools stickers on page 57 and 58.

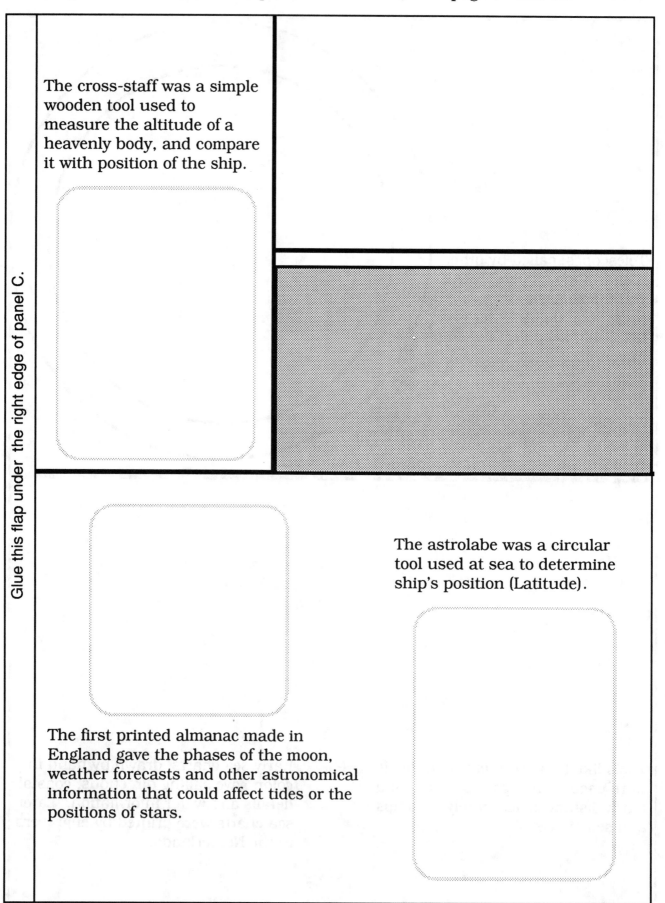

Glue this flap under the right edge of panel C.

The cross-staff was a simple wooden tool used to measure the altitude of a heavenly body, and compare it with position of the ship.

The astrolabe was a circular tool used at sea to determine ship's position (Latitude).

The first printed almanac made in England gave the phases of the moon, weather forecasts and other astronomical information that could affect tides or the positions of stars.

Social Skills: Ask for help, explain answers, seek accuracy.
Academic Skills: Create and compare simple classroom maps.
Teacher: Before you begin the activity, clearly mark the North, South, East and West of your room. Reproduce a map grid for each student. (page 64) Have students make sure to turn their page so that the compass on their paper is in correct alignment to the classroom. Note: Younger students can concentrate on only the closest, or farthest points for their maps. Older students can add other layers of details to their maps.

MAKE-A-MAP

See your room from a different perspective.

Directions:

1. Turn your paper so that the N on your compass is facing NORTH.
2. Draw symbols of the closest things around you in the classroom on the NORTH, SOUTH, EAST and WEST.
3. Draw symbols of the farthest things away from you in the classroom on the NORTH, SOUTH, EAST AND WEST.
4. Put samples of the symbols in the key.
5. Use your maps to try the group Make-a-Map activities below.

Make-A-Map Activity Card 1: LET'S NAVIGATE!

Pick a destination you agree on. Using your map, write directions to get to it. Take time to read and try each other's directions. Do the directions take you to your goal?

Make-A-Map Activity Card 2: KEYS TO MAP MAKING!

Compare your maps to see what symbols you used in the keys. How are they alike? How are they different? Get out other maps to see what symbols are used. Make a chart showing some of the symbols you found and what they mean.

Make-A-Map Activity Card 3: MAP MIX-UP!

Put your completed maps in one pile, face down. Shuffle and pass out to members. Reading your map, try to find the desk locations it is showing. Did you find it? Discuss what confused or helped you.

Make-a-Map Grid Pattern

Use with the directions and the activity cards on page 63.

Map Key Suggestions:

⊟ bookcase   ⊢ doorway

⊔ desk   ♀ globe

▭ chalk board   ⌨ pencil sharpener

Draw things farthest away.

Draw things closest to you.

your desk

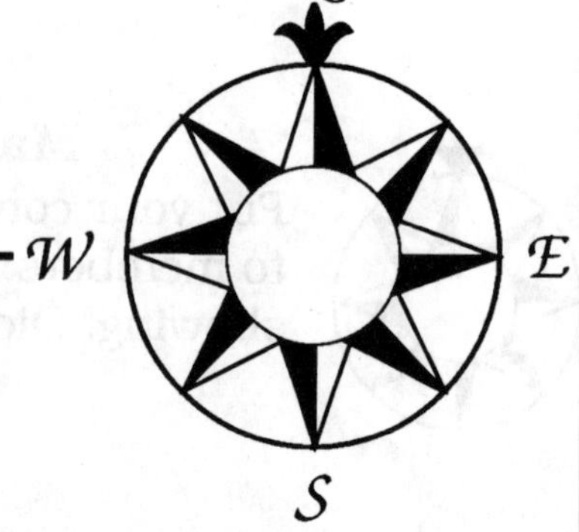

Map Key:

N

W   *E*

S

BOATSWAIN (BOSUN) CALL-TO-ORDER
Listen carefully to tune in to what's happening next!

CLASSROOM BOATSWAIN'S CALL CHART:

Our Meaning:	Explorer's Meaning:	Sound Patterns	
Gather in study groups.	Call Bosun's Mate.	high / low	- - - - - - - - - - -
Get your materials.	Haul or hoist.	high / low	⌐‾‾‾
Hand in assignments.	Belay.	high / low	∿∿∿
Gather in a large group.	Heave around the captain.	high / low	∿∿
Stop work or stand still.	Stop work or stand still.	high / low	————
Walk back.	Walk back.	high / low	∿∿∿∿∿∿
Go back to work.	Carry on.	high / low	‾‾⌐___
Clean up. Put away books.	Away boat.	high / low	⌐‾‾⌐___
Quiet, please.	Pipe down.	high / low	- - ∿∿___∿
Recess begins.	Breakfast or dinner.	high / low	∿∿___∿

Teacher Background: An early navigational tool developed in the Mediterranean was a WIND ROSE. It was one of the first compasses based on the Babylonian symbol of the sky as a circle, divided into equal sections. It showed the eight principal winds along with their halves and quarters. This sectioned the sky into 16 directions called "rhumbs of the wind" or "rhumbs." Mariners became accustomed to referring to directions as "winds." Later, the compass was further divided into 32 directions. The compass rose symbol was always shown as a key on maps and sea charts. A MAGNETIC COMPASS used by mariners (like those used today) was a wind rose with a magnetic needle suspended on top. Lodestone (a naturally magnetic mineral) was found to point to the north star when freely suspended. If held carefully, the compass made it possible for the proper wind directions to be determined at sea, even if the winds died down or the sky was cloudy.

RHUMBS OF THE WIND GAME

For best focus, do this activity indoors. This page has directions for making the floor compass rose. The following page has directions for playing the game. (Use a gymnasium floor or a corner of your classroom.)

Materials:
Two 6' lengths of 36" wide brown kraft paper
Masking tape
Yardstick
Wide-tipped black permanent marker
Crayons or colored markers (optional)
Small portable fan (with safety blades!)
12 ft. extension cord

Get ready. Create a giant floor compass rose:
1. Tape 2 pieces of 3' wide kraft paper together.
2. Put a yardstick in the middle of the paper; trace and cut out a 6' circle.
3. Write NORTH at the top of the taped line, and SOUTH at the bottom of the taped line, at the opposite end of the circle.
4. Fold the circle the opposite way. Label lines EAST and WEST as shown.
5. Hold the circle so that the folded lines become an "X". Fold in half. Fold the remaining half-circle in half. Unfold and label the lines NORTHEAST, NORTHWEST, SOUTHEAST, and SOUTHWEST as shown.
6. Mark an **X** in the center with an arrow toward NORTH.
7. The compass can be in decorated any way you'd like. Look at other compasses to see the star shapes inside and how they are designed.

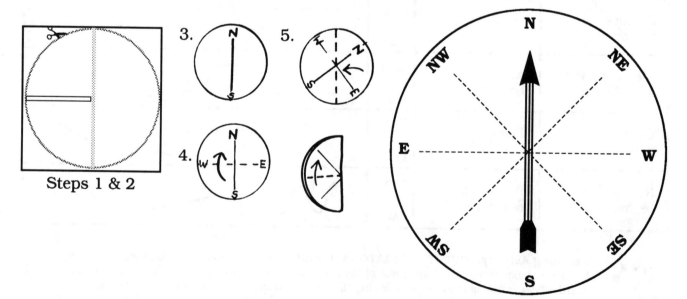

Steps 1 & 2

Finished Floor Compass

Social Skills: Speak clearly, ask for help when needed, explain answers.
Academic Skills: Feel and name wind directions.
Teacher: Children find wind directions with a sensory focus. Reproduce compass and arrrow on tag board. Ask a parent helper or older student to direct the pairs as they see and feel the directions of the wind. Note: A group can be assigned to prepare the hand-held compass below.

RHUMBS OF THE WIND GAME

Feel wind directions as you learn how to read a compass rose.

Materials:
Compass rose patterns
Brass brad

To Assemble the Compass Rose:
1. Color and cut out the compass and arrow.
2. Use a sharp pencil to punch a small hole in the centers of compass rose and arrow.
3. Place a brad through the arrow and the compass. Open prongs to secure.

To Play:
1. One player stands in the middle of the floor compass, holds the small compass rose, and faces NORTH.
2. A second player walks around the outside of the floor compass, then stops on one of the compass points. The fan is turned on and pointed toward the player in the center.
3. The child in the center turns the compass arrow toward the wind direction and names the direction of the wind. If the answer is right, the players trade places and try another direction. If not, the child on the edge moves and blows the "wind" from another point for the child in the middle to guess again.

Compass Rose Patterns

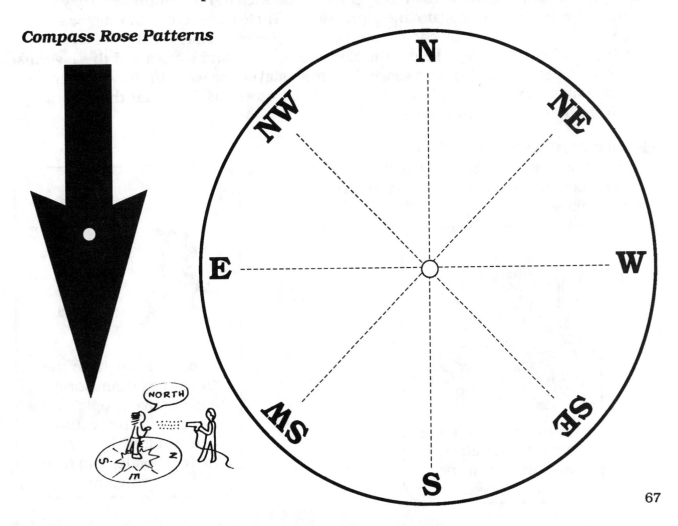

Chapter 5: The Legacy of Exploration

When explorers traveled away from their homelands, they found many cultures and ways of life different from their own. The people they met spoke in different languages, dressed differently, ate different foods, used different tools, and had different ideas about religion and family life.

As time passed, the explorers began to communicate with these peoples in the "new" lands. They took new plants, animals, medicines, and foods back to Europe with them. Most of these new things made European life better. Healthier foods kept people stronger. Medicines cured many of their ailments. Treasures, furs, and fine fabrics made them wealthier. The lives of the Europeans for the most part were better, more comfortable than they had been before they had these new goods.

European explorers also brought animals and plants from across the world to the Americas. Native peoples learned to ride horses. Cattle, hogs, and chickens were added to their food supply. New plants like coffee and sugarcane were planted. But for the most part, the lives of the people in America did not improve. They became laborers on vast sugar cane plantations. Their traditions and religious beliefs were changed, not by choice, but by force. Diseases like smallpox and measles had been unknown before the Europeans came and introduced these germs. More native peoples died from disease than from slavery or war. In this chapter we will learn about what the explorers brought to the Americas and what they brought back from the Americas to Europe.

TRICKY TRADERS STICK-ONS

Color, cut out, and add to the time line.
Use the stick-ons again with the Tricky Traders
Game on page 76.

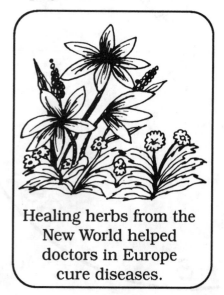

Healing herbs from the New World helped doctors in Europe cure diseases.

Horses brought to the Americas from Europe made native people's lives easier. They could travel farther, carry heavier loads, and hunt larger game.

CROSS-CULTURAL GIFT STICK-ONS

Color, cut out and add to the time line. Use the stickers on pages 69 and 70 to go with the Food-for-All Learning Baskets on page 75 and the Tricky Traders Game on page 76. (The words in parentheses tell where the item originated.)

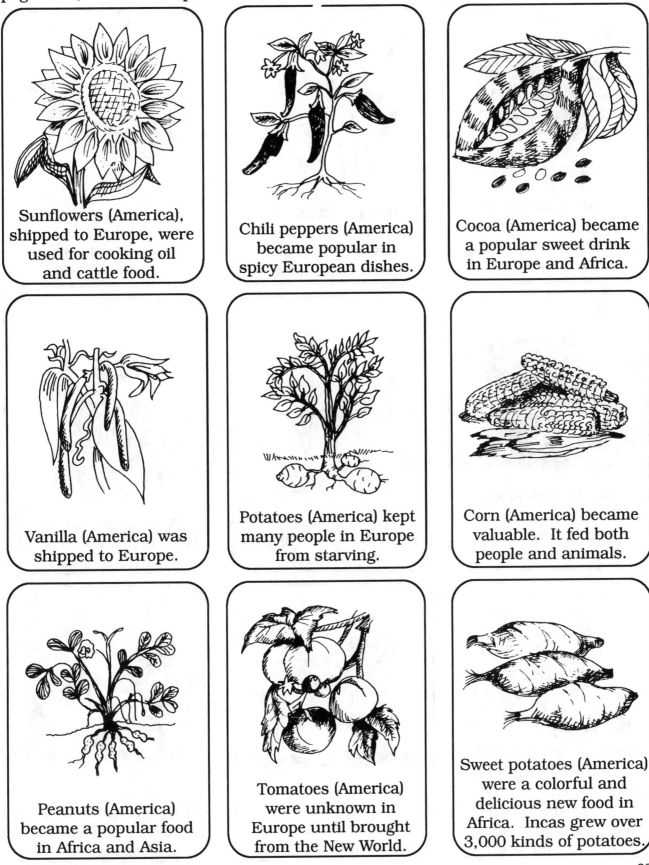

Sunflowers (America), shipped to Europe, were used for cooking oil and cattle food.

Chili peppers (America) became popular in spicy European dishes.

Cocoa (America) became a popular sweet drink in Europe and Africa.

Vanilla (America) was shipped to Europe.

Potatoes (America) kept many people in Europe from starving.

Corn (America) became valuable. It fed both people and animals.

Peanuts (America) became a popular food in Africa and Asia.

Tomatoes (America) were unknown in Europe until brought from the New World.

Sweet potatoes (America) were a colorful and delicious new food in Africa. Incas grew over 3,000 kinds of potatoes.

CROSS-CULTURAL GIFT STICK-ONS CONT'D.

Color, cut out and add to the time line. Use the stick-ons on page 69 and this page to go with the Food-for-All Learning Baskets on page 75 and the Tricky Traders Game on page 76.

Native Americans quickly learned to raise the chickens brought over from Spain.

Grains such as oats, barley, and rye grew well in cooler parts of America.

Hogs were brought to America in the 1400's and grew well.

Coffee (Africa) became popular in America. South Americans learned to grow it.

Sugar cane (Africa) grew well in America.

Pineapples from the West Indies were traded to Africa and India.

Turkeys were traded by the Aztecs to Europe. Pilgrims brought them back to America and were surprised to find them in the wild.

Sheep from Europe helped Incas in Peru.

Pumpkins from the New World made European meals tastier.

Social Skills: Form groups quietly, participate, ask for help.
Academic Skills: Create classroom demonstrations of trade goods from the age of exploration.
Teacher: Students go to an area of interest, then work together to create group projects featuring edible displays, games, or hands-on lessons. Note: Plan to give extra help to the groups or have a parent on hand to guide their efforts.

Extending Activity: TEAM EXCHANGE Students take turns demonstrating what they have done and how it is used. The Food-for-All poster and Tricky Traders Game activities can become part of a classroom display for children to use in their free time. Reproduce extra recipe cards to be kept on hand for students to try at home.

THE GREAT EXCHANGE
FOOD FOR THOUGHT—AND FOR EATING!
(International Foods and Recipes)

Use the lists below to gather foods for the recipes on pages 73 and 74. Group members can contribute most of them. Note: Check recipes for measurements, cooking, and serving utensils.

NATIVE AMERICAN PEANUT SOUP INGREDIENTS:
> chunky peanut butter
> chicken broth
> milk
> chives (fresh, frozen, or dried)

WEST INDIES PINEAPPLE DIP INGREDIENTS:
> 1 fresh pineapple
> 1 carton sour cream
> 1 jar coconut cream
> brown sugar

EUROPEAN POTATO DUMPLINGS INGREDIENTS:
> frozen potato patties, thawed
> all-purpose flour
> salt
> pepper
> nutmeg
> 1 egg

SPICY MEXICAN CHOCOLATE INGREDIENTS:
> hot cocoa mix
> ground cinnamon
> ground nutmeg
> vanilla extract
> cinnamon sticks

A PECK OF PEPPERS INGREDIENTS:
Gather a variety of hot and mild peppers (red, green, yellow, etc.)

THINKING AND MANIPULATING
Gifts of Civilization Activities

Use the lists below to organize materials for the games on the following pages. They will help you be sure each group has everything needed for a project.

FOOD-FOR-ALL LEARNING BASKETS
Materials List:
- Stick-Ons, pages 69 and 70
- Food-For-All Basket Tags, page 75
- Crayons
- Scissors, glue
- 4 pieces of yarn cut in 4" lengths
- 18 pieces of yarn cut in 18" lengths
- 4 small baskets with handles (Easter-type baskets)

TRICKY TRADERS GAME
Materials List:
Note: Copy the first five materials on oaktag. The cards are not all the same size
- 1 set of Gifts of Civilization co-op cards, pages 78, 79, 80
- 1 set of Stick-Ons, pages 68, 69, 70
- 1 set Trade Cards, page 77
- 1 Merchant Ship Game Board pattern, page 76. Copy 1 per player
- 1 Merchant Mania Cube pattern, page 77. Make 1 per game
- Construction paper
- Scissors
- Crayons

DEAL & FEEL AND DEAL & TAKE GAMES
Materials List:
- 1 set Gifts of Civilization co-op cards page 78, 79, 80
- Small cloth swatches: wool, cotton, silk
- Spice samples (cinnamon stick, peppercorns, etc.)
- Small bundles or bags of grains
- Small packages of dried corn, barley, etc.
- Plastic or real fruits (apple, pineapple, etc.)
- Plastic model of fish or picture of fish
- Small piece of fake fur
- Metal objects (gold, silver, iron, steel, etc.)
- Cardboard boot box (1 per game)
- Envelope
- Masking tape
- Scissors

Social Skills: Use names, paraphrase, listen actively.
Academic Skills: Find, read and prepare international recipes.
Teacher: Help organize materials. All cooking activities should be closely supervised. Pairs will make each different dish, but have everyone try the results. Note: If portions are made smaller, perhaps the whole class can have just a "taste".

FOOD FOR THOUGHT RECIPES

NATIVE AMERICAN PEANUT SOUP

8-10 servings

This recipe from *Native American Recipes for the Classroom* by Dr. Karen Harvey of Littleton, Ohio is used with permission.

Ingredients:
8 oz. chunky peanut butter
2 cups chicken broth
2 cups milk
1 TBL chopped fresh or dried chives

Utensils: wooden spoon, spatula, measuring spoons and cup, large pot, ladle
Cook: In crock pot, on hot plate, or stove top
Serve: In small hot/cold cups, with plastic spoons

Partner Directions:
Partner 1: Put peanut butter in pot.
Partner 2: Put chicken broth in pot. Stir well.
Partner 1: Put chives and milk in pot. Stir well.
Partner 2: Stir while heating. Serve in small cups.

WEST INDIES PINEAPPLE DIP

8-10 servings

Other fresh fruit can be used for this recipe, too!

Ingredients:
1 fresh pineapple cut into pieces
2/3 cup dairy sour cream
1/3 cup coconut cream (purchase bottled or canned)
1/3 cup brown sugar

Utensils: Mixing (serving) bowl, measuring cup, spoon, plate for fruit
Cook: No cooking needed, but will need to be refrigerated
Serve: On small paper plates: Use toothpicks to spear and dip fruit

Partner Directions:
Partner 1: Put sour cream and coconut cream in a bowl. Stir.
Partner 2: Add brown sugar to mixture. Stir.
Partner 1: Arrange pineapple on a serving plate.
Partner 2: Put a toothpick in each piece of fruit for dipping.

EUROPEAN POTATO DUMPLINGS
6-8 servings
For safety an adult should do the cooking, as boiling water is needed.

Ingredients:
1 pkg. (12 oz.) frozen potato patties, thawed
1/3 cup unsifted all-purpose flour (set a little more aside, too)
1 tsp. salt
1/8 tsp. pepper
1/4 tsp. nutmeg
1 egg, beaten
2 quarts boiling water

Utensils: Fork, mixing bowl, measuring spoons and cup, large pot, lid, slotted spoon
Cook: In 2 quarts boiling water on stove or hot plate, drain on paper towels
Serve: On small paper plates with plastic forks: Butter is nice on top!

Partner Directions:
Partner 1: Put patties in bowl and break them up with a fork.
Partner 2: Add flour and egg to patties. Stir.
Partner 1: Add nutmeg, salt, and pepper to mixture. Stir.
Partners 1 and 2: Shape dough into 6-8 balls. Roll in flour and set aside.
Parent: Drop the dumplings into boiling water and cover. Cook for 18-20 minutes.

SPICY MEXICAN CHOCOLATE
An adult should pour the hot water; students add their own spices!

Ingredients:
Hot cocoa mix
1 cup hot water per person
dash cinnamon
dash nutmeg
drop vanilla extract
cinnamon sticks (1 per serving)

Utensils: Saucepan, measuring cup, and spoon
Cook: Coffee maker can heat water for mixing cocoa; no other cooking is needed
Serve: In small hot/cold cups

A PECK OF PEPPERS
Be very careful about touching or tasting hot peppers! They can burn fingers, tongues, and eyes!

Ingredients:
Gather a variety of hot and mild
peppers: red, green, yellow, etc.
for children to view or sample.

Social Skills: Work toward a goal, participate, seek accuracy.
Academic Skills: Match food lists with facts.
Teacher: Children will add movable food items to baskets. As they read a tag, they move the food to another basket. When all the foods are distributed, children can see at a glance the yarn strings trailing basket to basket. Simple trade routes! Reproduce a set of Food Stickers and Basket Tags. Set aside with the other materials listed on pages 69–70. Students divide tasks listed among group members to complete the activity.

FOOD-FOR-ALL LEARNING BASKETS

The foods that were exchanged during the years of trade and exploration that began in 1492 made a big difference in people's lives. This activity will help you see how foods were shared around the world.

Food-For-All Basket Tags:

○ **North America and Mexico**

sunflowers	vanilla
cocoa	corn
turkeys	herbs

○ **Europe**

barley	rye
cows	wheat
oats	hogs
chickens	horses

○ **South America and the West Indies**

potatoes	sweet potatoes
corn	tobacco
peanuts	tomatoes
pineapples	chili peppers

○ **Africa**

coffee	sugar

Food-For-All Tasks:
1. Cut out the basket tags and attach one to each basket with a 4" piece of yarn.
2. Cut an 18" yarn piece for each food listed on the tags. Tie that number of yarn pieces to the basket handle.
3. Cut out and color the food stickers.
4. Attach one food sticker to each yarn string, following the list on the tag.
5. Arrange the four baskets on a table as shown in the diagram, 12 inches apart.

To Play:
Start at one basket. Read the message on each food card and move it over to the basket where the food was taken. Each group member reads and moves a food tag until all the baskets have been completed.

Note: The yarn strings from basket to basket are like the early trade routes the explorers used! There is more than one way to complete this activity, so put the foods back to their original baskets and try it again! A different destination will make new trade routes.

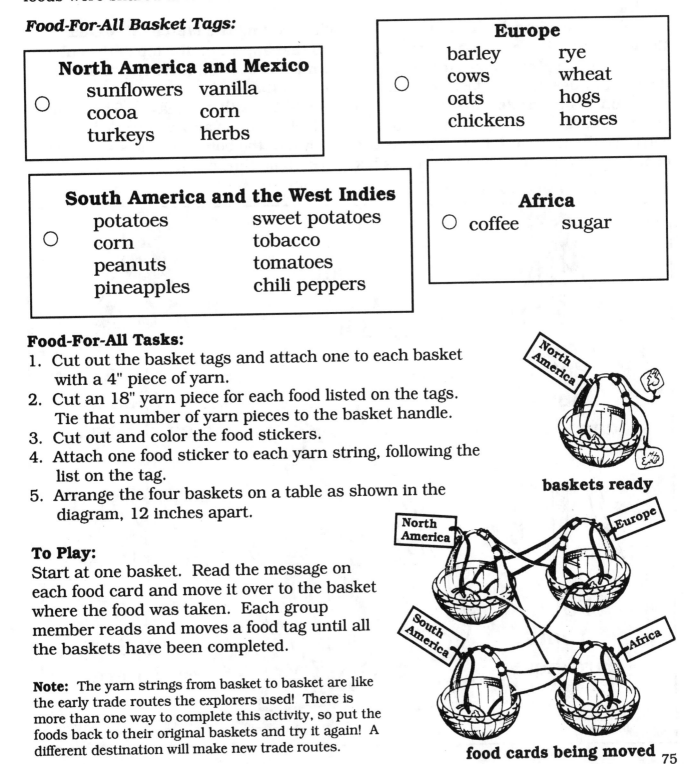

baskets ready

food cards being moved

Social Skills: Use names, listen actively, check answers.
Academic Skills: Recognize and compare categories of goods and products.
Teacher: Reproduce all game materials on tag board. The game works for 2-6 players. Copy one Merchant Ship Game Board for each player. Reproduce 1 set of Trade Cards from page 77 for 2-4 players, and 2 sets for 4-6 players. Make one Merchant Mania Cube for each game.

TRICKY TRADERS GAME

Get Ready:
1. Cut out the cards. Shuffle the Trade Cards into the co-op cards. Stack face down in the middle of the playing area.
2. Cut out and assemble the Merchant Mania Game Cube following the directions.

To Play:

Take turns **choosing a card** from the stack or **rolling the Merchant Mania Cube**. If you roll the cube, follow the directions that appear on the top of the cube. If you choose a **gifts** co-op card, place it on your game board if there is a place for it. If you can't use it, put it face down in the bottom of the stack.

If you draw a **trade** card, make the trade suggested with any player. Then put the trade card face down in the bottom of the stack. If the player you traded with can't use the new card, he or she puts it face down in the bottom of the stack. Play continues clockwise until a player has his or her game card filled.

Merchant Ship Game Board

Trade fabric for food.	**Trade animals for fabric.**	**Trade food for fuel.**
Trade tools for medicine.	**Trade animals for tools.**	**Trade medicine for fabric.**

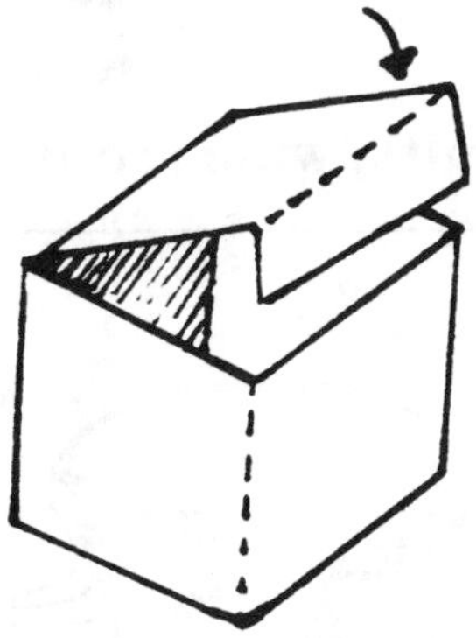

Merchant Mania Cube

tuck flap inside

Pirates Attack! Remove one card.

Land Sighted! Take another card.	**Wind's Gone!** Remove one card.	**Ship's Sinking!** Remove one card.	**Mutiny!** Remove one card.	tuck flap inside

Wind's Up! Take another card.

tuck flap inside

To Make Merchant Mania Cube:
1. Cut out the cube.
2. Fold on dotted lines.
3. Tuck small flaps inside cube.
4. Tape edges to secure.

Gifts of Civilization Co-op Cards

Use with Tricky Traders Game on 76 and Deal & Feel Games on page 80.

spices (Asia, West Indies)

nuts (America)

wheat (Europe)

fish (Europe)

fruits, wine (Europe)

oranges (Europe)

onions (Europe)

squash (America)

cattle (Europe)

peaches (Europe)

donkeys (Europe)

oxen (Europe)

Gifts of Civilization Co-op Cards
Use with Tricky Traders Game on 76 and Deal & Feel Games on page 80.

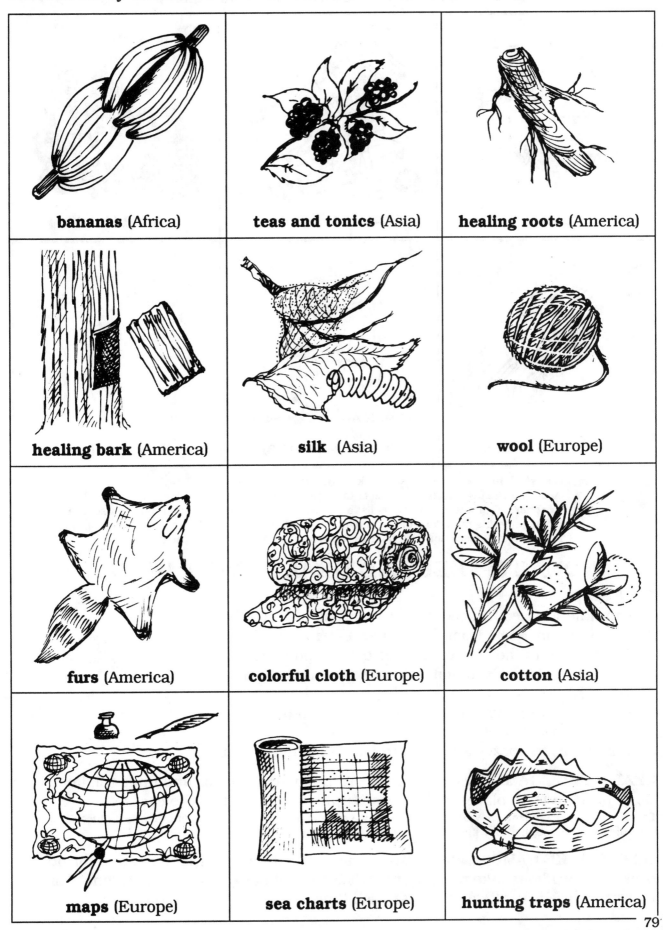

bananas (Africa)

teas and tonics (Asia)

healing roots (America)

healing bark (America)

silk (Asia)

wool (Europe)

furs (America)

colorful cloth (Europe)

cotton (Asia)

maps (Europe)

sea charts (Europe)

hunting traps (America)

Use with Tricky Traders Game on 76 and Deal & Feel Games on page 80.

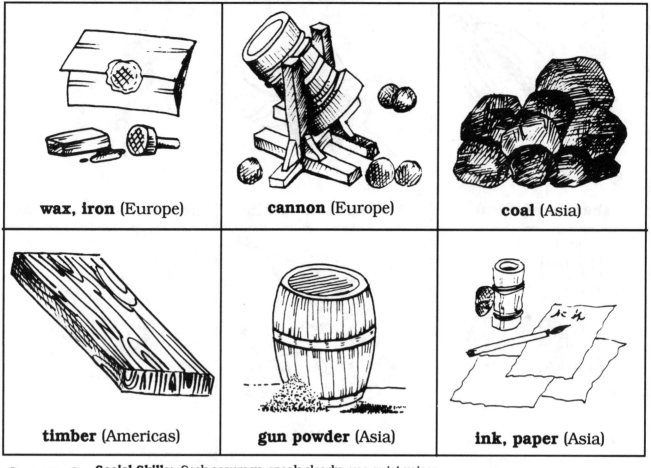

wax, iron (Europe) **cannon** (Europe) **coal** (Asia)

timber (Americas) **gun powder** (Asia) **ink, paper** (Asia)

Social Skills: Seek accuracy, speak clearly, use quiet voices.
Academic Skills: Recognize objects through touch.
Teacher: Reproduce a materials list and a set of co-op cards for each group to use as a guide when gathering materials for the activity. Even though the words are similar, each group should find different objects for their boxes. Groups switch boxes to play the game.

DEAL & FEEL AND DEAL & TAKE GAMES

Get Ready:
1. Cut a hand-sized "hinged door" in one end of a boot box.
2. Gather many items from the master materials list (pg. 72).
   Put them into the boot box. Tape the box lid down.
3. Choose co-op cards to match the items. Place them in a stack
   near the box.
4. Attach an envelope to the box top to store co-op cards when
   not in use.
5. Trade finished boxes and work in pairs to play the games.

DEAL & FEEL GAME: Read the cards. Your partner feels for and finds the item.
Don't peek! Switch places to do it again until you've used all the cards.
Teacher: Younger students may benefit from having a sample piece of fabric, bark or other item glued to the back of their card, so that they know what they are "feeling" for.

DEAL & TAKE GAME (easier): Make the door a little bigger (still covered for no peeking). Students take the object they've guessed out of the box each time. This way, there are fewer items to guess each time.

Chapter 6: Exploration in Literature and the Arts

During the years that the European explorers sailed to all areas on the globe, many cultures flourished. Tenochtitlán, the Aztec city, had about 100,000 people. Its streets were decorated with sculptures, grand palaces, and temples.

China had been ruled by the Ming Dynasty since 1368. Peking was the center of culture, where artists and architects built the "Forbidden City" with its beautiful pagodas, waterways, and courtyards. The Chinese were also famous for beautiful landscapes painted on silk and for fine porcelain vases and dishes.

In Africa many cultures existed. Benin, the capital city of the Bini, was one of the most important cultural and commercial centers of western Africa. The Bini had no written language, but European explorers wrote of their culture and traditions. The Bini had large bronze plaques that pictured their ways of life and religion. In 1520 the Europeans were especially surprised to find pious Christians in Ethiopia. These people had been Christians since 333 A.D. Lalibela had once been Ethopia's capital. It still has ten churches that were carved underground within solid rock. The workers chipped down into the rock until they had dug a trench forty feet deep. Then they carved the rock into the shape of a Greek cross and hollowed it out into a church.

In this chapter, you will be touching on some of the art and literature from around the world during the age of exploration. Try to see the many differences and similarities in the art of different cultures. Peoples from around the world have expressed their love for art and history in many beautiful ways.

Art and Literature Stick-Ons
Color, cut out, and add to the time line.

1368 Ming Dynasty begins in China.

1492 The Ethiopian king, "Conquering Lion of Judah," receives an ambassador from Portugal.

1452 Leonardo Da Vinci, famous painter and sculptor, is born.

ART AND LITERATURE STICK-ONS

Color, cut out, and add to the time line. Note: Make and keep an extra set of these stickers to use with the Museum Curator activity on page 84.

1000 Japanese female author, Murasaki Shikubu writes the world's first novel, *The Tale of Genji*.

1400 Geoffrey Chaucer writes the book, *Canterbury Tales*.

1375 The legend of Robin Hood begins to appear in English literature.

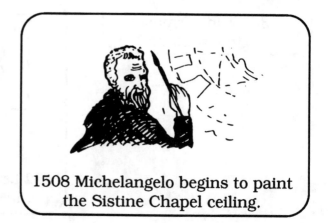

1508 Michelangelo begins to paint the Sistine Chapel ceiling.

1570 Glassmaking is a fine art in Europe.

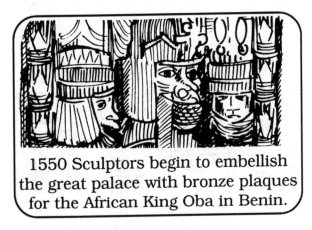

1550 Sculptors begin to embellish the great palace with bronze plaques for the African King Oba in Benin.

1070 As-Bakri, a Spanish-Arab geographer, writes *Book of Roads and Kingdoms* about the splendors of African kings.

1000 Chinese porcelain is known for its excellence throughout Asia.

1470 Florentine merchants visit the palaces of Timbuktu, the intellectual capital of Western Sudan in Africa.

Social Skills: Integrate ideas, jog memory, use names.
Academic Skills: Learn and recognize places and art forms from different cultures.
Teacher: Reproduce a set of cards for each pair to use together. Pairs can also group the cards by country, type of card, or Old World/New World.
Teacher Background: The age of exploration was an exciting time for the world. As explorers brought back stories of other places and cultures, people began to realize that civilizations shared many things in common: Religions and places of worship, a need for creative expression in word, song and art, and the use of symbols to show their beliefs or identity.

ART-I-FACTS

Learn about other cultures and their civilizations! Cut out the co-op cards. Show them to your partner and talk about them together.

Social Skills: Integrate ideas, jog memory, speak clearly.
Academic Skills: Learn about and describe places and art forms from different cultures.
Teacher: Reproduce a set of Art-I-Fact Cards (pages 85 and 86) on oaktag for each group. Provide each group with an 11"x17" piece of drawing paper.

MUSEUM CURATOR GAME

Get Ready: Cut out the Art-I-Fact Cards. With your group, pick out 6-10 cards that you would like to include in your "museum". Decorate your piece of drawing paper with frames, pedestals and easels to look like an art gallery. Add a dotted outline for each card needed (inside the frames, on top of the pedestals, etc.) on the paper. Fill out a Museum Card like the one below for each piece of art in your gallery. Place it near the art.

Museum Card

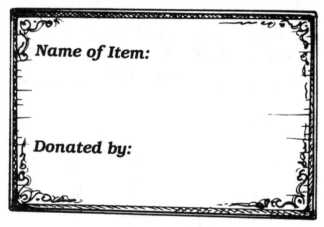

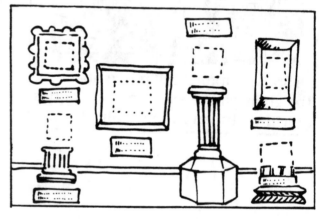

To Play: Place the co-op cards on a table, near the museum. One group member at a time gives a "tour" of the museum, telling about each item (where it was found, and why it was picked for this museum, and what makes it important). The other players find and match the co-op cards. Play the game a number of times, each time with a different curator. You can share other facts you may have learned about each artifact when you give a "tour."

Extending Activity: ART DEALERS Use the Art-I-Fact Cards with the Tricky Traders Game on page 76. Make an extra set of the Trading cards and game boards. Blank out the the old categories and write in the new categories (religious place or symbol, book or statue, special building) on the merchant ship game cards. The Merchant Mania Cube will be fine for this game as well.

Aztec Temple

Chinese Pagoda

African Church

French Church

Italian Statue

Mayan Stele

African Statue

Chinese Buddha

African Mask

Aztec Mosaic Mask

Italian Mask

Chinese Mask

African Headdress

Spanish Crown

Mayan Headdress

Aztec Painting

Chinese Sculpture

Da Vinci Painting

African Carving

Aztec Calendar

English Chalice

Aztec Vessel

African Headrest

Chinese Vase

Social Skills: Criticize ideas, not people, plan aloud, work together toward a goal.
Academic Skills: Plan and complete a mosaic "relic."
Teacher: Use the patterns provided, or have older children make their own outline drawing to use. Note: Art needs to be simple. You can have each group work on 1-4 patterns at a time, depending on the speed and activity each can handle with control. Children may want to practice glueing on scrap paper before glueing their final project.

PAPER PLATE MOSAICS
Discover an historical art form!

Many cultures from around the world have used mosaics as an art form to express events in history or religious beliefs.

Materials Needed:
Mosaic patterns (1-4 per group) or simple drawings
4 colors of construction paper (cut into 4 x 6 pieces)
glue
1 paper plate for each mosaic

Roundtable Directions:
Partner 1: Pass out construction paper (1 color per member).
Partner 2: Choose a pattern with your group. Glue it to the paper plate.
Partner 3: Plan how the pattern will be colored by asking each member what area they think their color should be. Put your initials on the areas you will color. Make sure it is pretty equal and all agree.
All: Tear your piece of colored paper into 1/4" sized "mosaic" pieces.
All: Spread glue in one area of your picture, then fill it in with the torn pieces. Leave a little white area between each piece so that the shapes will stand out. Fit the pieces like a loose puzzle. Pass it on.
All: Take turns filling in the pattern. Keep filling in one area at a time and passing until all the parts are filled in.
Partner 4: Glue a decorative border with leftover pieces of construction paper to accent the mosaic colors in the pattern. Make sure everyone in your group signs it.

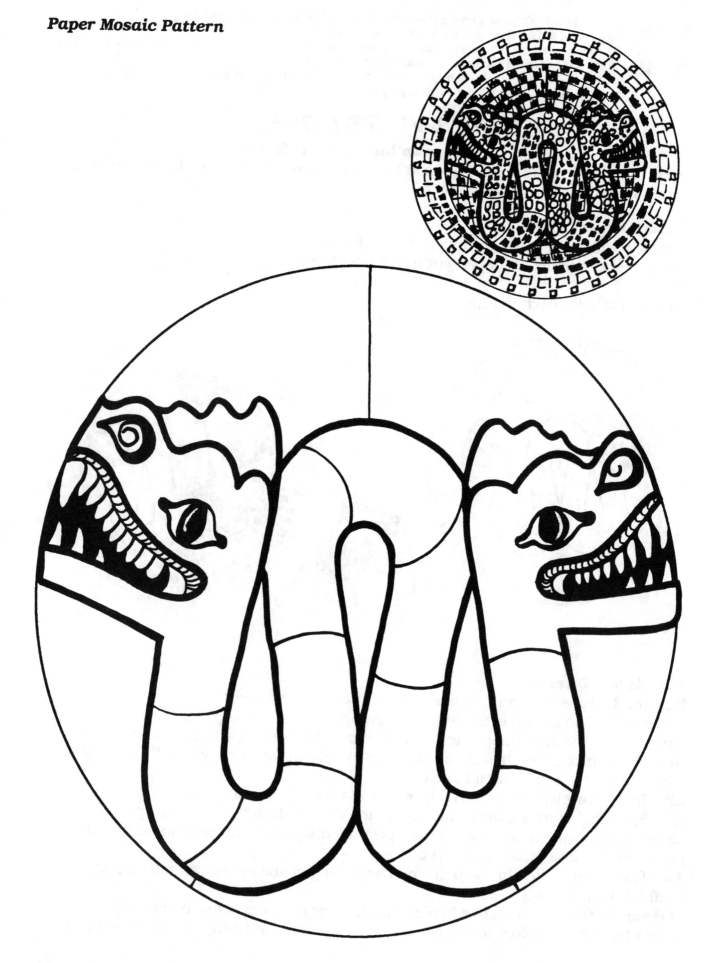

Social Skills: Work together, check for accuracy.
Academic Skills: Reading, listing characters, creating an original story.
Teacher: Gather copies of *Doctor Coyote* and *Aesop's Fables* for groups to use. Explain that both groups of stories have morals, a lesson to be learned from the tale.

DOCTOR COYOTE
A Native American Aesop's Fables

An early copy of *Aesop's Fables* was taken to Mexico after the Spanish conquest. An Aztec scribe translated them and adapted them to Native American Coyote stories, familiar to many native peoples at the time. Enjoy reading the stories in *Doctor Coyote* and work through the activities below with your partner.

Compare a Fable

Read a story from *Doctor Coyote*. Find an Aesop's fable that tells a similar story. Make a poster comparing the characters in the Aesop's fable and the characters in the Coyote story. How were the morals in each story similar or different?

Create a Fable

After reading several stories in *Doctor Coyote* and several *Aesop's Fables*, create your own fable with a moral at the end. Use the Coyote characters below to create a scene from your fable. Be ready to tell your fable and show your picture to other groups.

Doctor Coyote Stand-Up Characters

89

Social Skills: Extend another's answer, elaborate, work together.
Academic Skills: Reading, sharing and re-telling myths.
Teacher: Reproduce story cards and imagination strips for your class. Pairs choose a story and strip to use. Provide art materials for children to use to create imaginative drawings, posters or displays to illustrate their stories. Background notes are given for each story to introduce it. Gather other materials to expand myths and stories.

LEARN-A-LEGEND
Story Cards with Ancient Myths to Read and Share

Choose an imagination-starter strip for your story card. Fill in the name or glue it to a larger paper to make your own adventure story. When your story is done, work with your partner to create an imaginative poster or display to go along with it. To learn more about myths the explorers knew, read *The Life Treasury of American Folklore* © 1961 by Time, Inc.

Imagination-Starter Strips
Use with **Story Cards.**

At last! We could see golden rooftops of a beautiful city ahead.
We heard strange music as our ship inched along the foggy shoreline.
As we traveled, we dreamed of the day we'd find ....

Story Cards

Mermaids Story Card
Background: On long voyages many sailors believed they sighted mermaids in the mists and fogs along seacoasts. They were sighted in many places by the early navigators.

Mermaids
Mermaids appeared to be beautiful women with long, golden hair. From the waist down they resembled fish. The would perch on rocks along a seacoast. Mermaids combed their hair with gold combs and sang lovely songs that entranced sailors to join them under the sea. It was said that sailors and mermaids raised families there.

The homes of the mermaids were under the ocean in a vast city of grottoes lighted by crystal pyramids. There were gardens of brightly colored seaweed. Furniture was of amber. Floors were iridescent pearls. Diamonds and rubies were everywhere.

Saint Elmo's Fire Story Card

Background: St. Elmo was a bishop in the fourth century. Later he became the patron saint of sailors on the Mediterranean Sea. The "fire" would cause the tips of masts and spars to glow. It was actually a discharge of electricity which caused the glowing effect. When they saw St. Elmo's fire, sailors believed the saint would protect them during a storm. Note: This story is taken from Columbus's journal during his second voyage.

Saint Elmo's Fire

On Saturday, at night, the body of St. Elmo was seen, with seven lighted candles in the round top, and there followed mighty rain and frightful thunder.

I mean the lights were seen which the seamen affirm to be the body of St. Elmo, and they sang litanies and prayers to him looking upon it as most certain that in these storms, when he appears, there can be no danger. Whatever this is I leave to others, for, if we may believe Pliny, when such lights appeared in those times to Roman sailors in a storm, they said they were Castor and Pollux.

Quivira Story Card

Background: The Turk told many stories of Quivira to Coronado. The Turk knew that he could never fight Coronado and win. He wanted to somehow trick Coronado out in the wilderness because he wanted to live in his little "iron house" (Coronado's gilded armor). Coronado believed the exaggerated stories of the fabulous city because he desperately wanted to find their riches.

The Turk's Quivira

Quivira is a large city where gold and jewels abound. Even the servants of the king wear jeweled headbands, earrings, and necklaces. Their clothes are adorned with colorful feathers from exotic birds. The king naps each day under a tree. The tree is decorated with many golden bells. The bells gently chime in the breeze and lull the king into a peaceful sleep.

Social Skills: Participate, use quiet voices, work toward common goal.
Academic Skills: Make a cut and paste ocean myth scene.
Teacher: Reproduce one top and bottom sheet for each pair to complete. Note: Younger students may need help cutting and folding the windows on the top sheet.

LIFT-AND-SEE MONSTERS

The sailors who explored the Atlantic had many fears about what the ocean was like. Beyond the Azores there was little knowledge of what to expect. Many tales of monsters and other dangers fueled the imaginations of frightened sailors as they began their journeys into the unknown.

Lift-and-See Bottom Sheet

Place glue around outside edges.

To Make:

1. Color the top and bottom sheets.
2. Cut the windows carefully.
3. Carefully add glue around edges of bottom sheet.
4. Place top sheet down and let dry.
5. Open the windows for a deep sea surprise.

Lift and See Top Sheet

Extending Activity: DRAW-AND-SEE-MONSTERS Use just the top sheet with blank paper below to make original sea monster drawings to make another surprise ocean scene. Note: For this version, cut and open the windows before gluing, then draw inside the open spaces. When drawing is done, and glue is dry, close the windows to open and look. Exchange with other groups.

Social Skills: Summarize material, praise others, ask for help, integrate ideas into one.
Academic Skills: Plan and create puppet plays featuring lives of explorers.
Teacher: Each group plans a simple play featuring an event in the life of an explorer using any of the puppets shown (pp. 96-97). Have them fill out the planner page to see what they will need and plan who will do each part of the production. Reproduce puppets on tag board. Make the patterns and directions available for them to create their own scenes. Plan to have the materials left out on display for other children to use to create spontaneous playlets or re-creations of the original

PAPER BAG PUPPETS AND PLAYS

❦ ❦ ❦ ❦ ❦ **Paper Bag Play Planner** ❦ ❦ ❦ ❦ ❦

Play Title: _____

Story Ideas: _____

_____

_____

Puppets Needed: _____

_____

Stage Settings and Art Ideas for Scenes: _____

_____

_____

_____

_____

_____

Note: Write your play on a separate paper or record it on an audio cassette.

Puppet Directions:
1. Choose the puppets you need for your play.
2. Color them with crayons or markers.
3. Cut along the outlines.
4. Glue a wooden stick to the back of each puppet as shown.
5. Write the puppet's name on its wooden stick.

To Use Puppets with the Paper Bag Stage:
Hold the puppets from the top. Move the puppets down into the bag from the top, or around the outside of the bag. Turn the bag to another side for other scenes.

Paper Bag Stage Materials:
2 large brown paper grocery bags
ruler
pencil
scissors
glue
poster paints or markers
old magazines

Paper Bag Stage Directions:
1. Cut apart one paper bag to have panels to glue over the printed sides of the other bag. Glue them in place to cover all the lettering.
2. When the glue has set on the "stage bag" panels, fold the top down one inch. Fold down again. This makes it sturdier on top.
3. Cut a front opening as shown. Fold the doors open.
4. Decide what setting you will need for your play. Decorate the stage with paints, markers, or use cut outs from old magazines to create castles, ships, or outdoor scenes. Use the front of the bag for one scene, the back of the bag for another. You can also have smaller scenes shown on the side panels. Make your paper bag stage interesting inside and out!

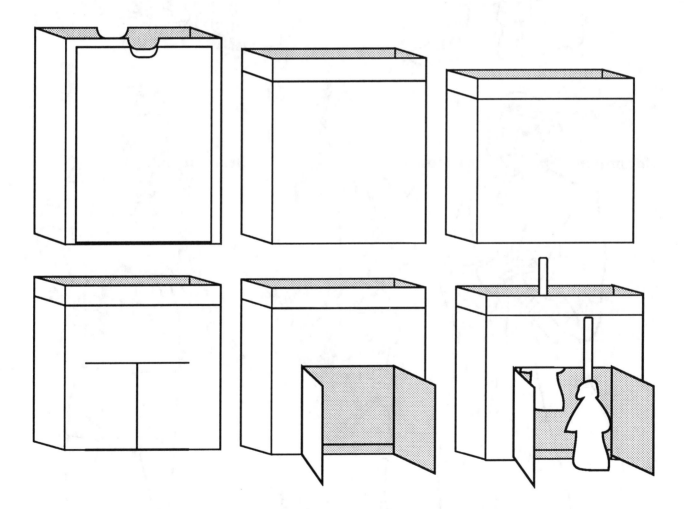

 Extending Activity: PICK UP AND PLAY Groups take the bags and puppets on portable puppet shows to other classrooms and perform them as a special treat for other classmates.

Puppets for
Paper Bag Plays

Marco
Polo

Ming,
Emperor of
China

Columbus

Coronado

Seaman

96

Puppets for Paper Bag Plays

Montezuma

Doña Marina

Headdress for Montezuma

Add crowns to Woman and Merchant to make them king and queen.

Woman

Merchant

Cortés

Appendix

AN OVERVIEW OF COOPERATIVE LEARNING

What makes cooperative learning unique?

In a cooperative classroom, group activities are more than just children working together. Learning structures (called recipes here) guide children to respond to and interact with each other in specific ways. Every task has both an academic and social goal, which are evaluated at the end of the activity with self-monitoring as well as teacher observation.

Instead of competition, students working together learn positive interdependence, that they sink or swim together. Each student contributes their part to each activity or assignment. Each team gets a single grade based on all the members doing their part. Instead of a few top students being the stars, all members must learn and use the information for the group to be successful. Students even take on the role of instructor, presenting new material or helping teammates practice skills.

The benefits of cooperative learning:

In a cooperative classroom, you become a facilitator to learning, not the prime source of instruction. Students begin to see their classmates as important and valuable sources of knowledge. Essential interpersonal social skills learned step by step and reinforced in every lesson make the classroom climate more positive, more nurturing, as students learn to give each other encouragement and praise.

Students even benefit academically, because in a cooperative atmosphere they have more chances to understand the material through oral rehearsal, thinking out loud, and discussing their views with others. Children learn that their differences make for a stronger team.

CLASSROOM GUIDELINES
GROUPING AND SOCIAL SKILLS

Planning for grouping and social skills:

Lessons have been planned for you so that the academic and social skills are built into the activity. This way, even if you have not worked with cooperative learning before, you can organize your groups quickly, spending your time monitoring and evaluating social progress.

Team groupings will be suggested for the activities. Primary classrooms work best in pairs because it is easier for children to decide or agree with one other person. Once they are working well in pairs, advance to threes and then two sets of pairs to make four. Unless your project demands it (such as a culminating activity having four or six distinct parts), four is the suggested upper limit for groups.

When choosing pairs, you may want to choose randomly or assign pairs to mix abilities and temperaments. Occasionally, you will find an oil-and-water pair, or a child who has trouble working with any partner and needs to be changed frequently. Once you have groups of four, make sure they are heterogeneous and have ample opportunity to "gel" as a group and learn to work together. Resist the temptation to break up groups who are having problems. Emphasize the social skills they need to learn and practice to get them all working together.

Defining and developing social skills:

Many teachers shy away from a group approach because they think of all the problems associated with groups of children working together: confusion, noise, personality conflicts, differences of opinion, etc. Cooperative teaching does not assume children have the social skills needed to work together successfully. The behaviors that enhance group progress are introduced, explained, modeled, practiced, and evaluated like any other skill.

To use cooperative learning successfully, it is important for you to be aware of the social skills appropriate for each activity. Introduce them at the beginning of each lesson, define, reinforce, and evaluate them at the completion of the assignment. As your groups develop, you may want to emphasize and build on other social skills of your choice. With older groups (grades 4—5), co-op activities are the ideal vehicle to experiment with learning and problem-solving skills. You can introduce these along with the simpler social skills.

These are the Interpersonal Group skills necessary in grades 1–5:

COMING TOGETHER (grades 1–5)
- form groups quietly
- stay in the group
- use quiet voices
- participate
- use names, make eye contact
- speak clearly
- listen actively
- allow no put-downs

WORKING TOGETHER (grades 1–5)
- work toward goal, purpose, time limit
- praise others, seek others' ideas
- ask for help when needed
- paraphrase other members' contributions
- energize group
- describe one's feelings when appropriate

LEARNING TOGETHER (grades 3–5)
- summarize material
- seek accuracy by correcting, giving information
- elaborate
- jog memory of teammates
- explain reasons for answers/beliefs
- plan aloud to teach concepts, agree on approaches

PROBLEM-SOLVING SKILLS (grades 4–5)
- criticize ideas, not people
- differentiate where there is disagreement
- integrate a number of ideas into a single conclusion
- ask for justification
- extend another's answer by adding to it
- probe by asking questions
- generate further answers
- check answers/conclusions with original instruction

Teaching social skills:
- Work on one social skill at a time. Add others slowly as groups are ready.
- Introduce the skill and discuss why it is important.
- Define in words and actions what children will see and hear as they are using that skill in their groups. Look through the materials in the classroom management sections to find charts, handouts, and other materials to help to do this.
- Give a demonstration for the children to follow (modeling).
- Set up practice situations and refer to the charts, etc., as children practice the skill.
- Praise lavishly attempts to use a skill, repeat words/deeds done showing it.
- At the end of the session, give children time to think whether they used the skill in the session or not. Evaluate them by the use of the teacher charts provided or have them vote as a group as to whether they think they succeeded and why.
- Be patient with yourself and the students. Social skills need to be practiced often to become natural.

COOPERATIVE GUIDELINES: PREPARING LESSONS

Along with the team grouping suggestions, cooperative recipes for learning (sometimes called practice structures) are used with the activities in this book. The symbol for the recipe is clearly shown on each lesson. The academic and social skills to be emphasized are beside each symbol. This will help you to organize the class and choose the lessons you wish to use.

The recipes provided each reinforce a number of social skills and guide children to process information in their groups in a variety of ways. For the first time through the materials, we suggest you use the recipe with one or two of the social skills listed near the symbols for each activity. However, when you are familiar with the projects, you can emphasize other skills. It is our hope that you will make the lessons your own, adapting them to your particular classroom. As you work through each, they will become natural to you and your students. They will make a positive impact on your classroom atmosphere and student performance. The key is to be patient and give children time to learn and practice each recipe.

COOPERATIVE CLASSROOM RECIPES

Sharing Circle

Social skills: Listen actively, participate, clear speech

Group size: Whole class

Directions: Children sit in a large circle, so each student can see the rest. The leader (teacher or student) starts an open-ended statement or sentence, and each student in turn ends it with their own statement. If they can't think of an answer at that time, they can pass, but are expected to have their answer ready by the time the circle is completed.

Round Robin

Social skills: Vocalization, time limit, quick associations, participate, extend another's answers, building team spirit

Group size: 3–4

Directions: This is an oral counterpart to Roundtable. **Note:** This is an excellent method for brainstorming vocabulary, problem solving, or creating an oral story together. It is also excellent for younger students with limited writing skills.

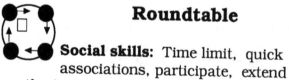

Roundtable

Social skills: Time limit, quick associations, participate, extend another's answers

Group size: 3–4

Directions: All team members contribute ideas to one sheet of paper. Make sure the team members know the directions the paper should be passed. When the signal is given, members write or draw the answer and pass it on.

Simultaneous Roundtable

Social skills: Time limit, waiting politely, quiet voices, participate

Group size: 3–4

Directions: More than one sheet is passed within the group. Members start with one sheet each and pass it on.

Study Group

Social skills: Paraphrasing, positive support, time limit, group purpose

Group size: 2–4

Directions: Present information in a traditional way. Children get into their small groups to complete a cooperative assignment that reinforces, expands on, or tests their knowledge. Groups can brainstorm, fill out a K W L chart within their groups to set goals for further study or complete various activities like word webbing. **Note:** Use the role cards and discussion strips to help keep social skills moving while in groups. Another quick associations recipe is **Numbered Heads Together.**

Numbered Heads Together

Social skills: Use quiet voices, participate, time limit, quick associations, elaborate, integration, team energizing, and praise

Group Size: 2–4

Note: For this activity, you will need a code or signal to get all the group's attention: lights on/off, a bell, or hand signal. Use it with other recipes as needed.

Directions: Students are in groups, listening to instruction by teacher. When a question is posed, the teacher tells the groups to put their heads together and discuss it. This gives students a chance to immediately discuss the information and figure out the right response together. After a time is given for discussion, the teacher signals for attention. At this time, students number off within each group. The teacher calls one number, and a representative from each group gives the team's answer. Team points are given for correct responses.

Note: If you want simultaneous responses, have team members write their response on a card and hold it up, or write their solution on the blackboard.

Interview

Social skills: Using names, eye contact, paraphrasing, summarizing, describing feelings, probing for answers, vocalization

Group size: 3–4

Note: This format is good to prepare for a unit or to close a unit.

Directions: Members take turns interviewing each other. After they have all had a chance to share, have the group round-robin what they learned from the interviews. For example, each child could take on one of the characters from an event or story and give his or her perspective. Use of role cards or discussion strips, so each asks a pertinent question, will help it go more smoothly.

Team Share

Social skills: Planning to teach, elaborate, vocalization, ways to jog memory, extend another's answers, integrate a number of ideas

Group size: 3–4

Note: This is an ideal way to have teams share products or projects with each other. Be sure to give teams time to plan how they will present themselves.

Directions: When teams have completed various projects, have them get ready to share with other teams. Organize the class so each team is clearly marked and knows where they are to go. For instance, a blue #1 card goes to one team, a blue #2 card goes to another, and they meet at the blue station. Team #1 shares first, team #2 is the audience. Then they switch. If you have an uneven number of teams, you can pair up with one or put three groups together.

Co-op Cards

Social skills: Using names, eye contact, positive statements, jog memory

Group size: Do first with partners, then in groups of 4.

Note: This format is an invaluable method for memory work and drill; children learn while praising each other and supporting each other's efforts.

Directions: Give each pair or study group a set of the Co-op Cards you want them to learn. Have them learn to play these games:

Game 1: Maximum Help
Partner 1 hands his card to partner 2. Partner 2, the teacher, shows the cards and the answers one by one, to Partner 1, the student, who repeats the words or answers. Cards done correctly are won back with lots of praise from the teacher. Cards done incorrectly are repeated and explained thoroughly by the tutor and asked again. When all cards are won back, they switch roles.

Game 2: Minimum Help
Partner 1 hands his card to partner 2. Partner 2, the teacher, shows the cards one by one to partner 1, the student, who answers. Cards done correctly are won back with lots of praise from the teacher. Cards done incorrectly are repeated with some hints. When all cards are won back, they switch roles.

Game 3: No Help
Partner 1 hands his card to partner 2. Partner 2, the teacher, shows the cards one by one to partner 1, the student, who answers. Cards done correctly are won back with lots of praise from the teacher. Cards done incorrectly are put back into the teacher's stack to be repeated with no hints. When all cards are won back, they switch roles.

Evaluation: Groups can keep a chart showing all words learned, with an envelope for those words that still need to be practiced and won.

Note: To keep the game fresh, the teacher should continually think of new and grander praises.

 ## Turn to Your Partner

Social skills: Using names, eye contact, listen actively, quiet voices, paraphrasing

Group size: 2

Directions: As you present material, have students pair up to share ideas, information, or opinions. This works best when you use established partners who sit near each other already, in order to minimize the amount of class time spent on moving toward partners. It is a good way to quickly reinforce active listening and early social skills.

Pairs Check or Partners

Social skills: Accuracy, energizing, positive support, ways to jog memory

Group size: 2

Directions: Teams work in pairs. In each pair, one player does a problem. The other is the coach in every sense of the word, giving help, praise, and encouragement! Switch roles after every problem. When two problems are completed, pairs must check with each other and agree on the answers. This is a good time to have a team handshake. Then proceed to the next two problems in the same way. Remember to keep your pairs heterogeneous for activities like this, so there is a range of abilities to keep things moving.

Think, Pair, Share, Think, Write, Pair, Share

Social skills: Paraphrasing, memory of content, vocalization

Group size: 2

Directions: Similar to Turn to Your Partner, but when more time is wanted on task. Present material, have students pair up to think about the content just presented, share ideas, information or opinions. This works well when you use established partners, but can also be used to exchange pairs to get different opinions. If you have children write down their idea (and it is a good idea, so they won't be swayed or lose direction), you can pair them up with others who think the same thing or have different opinions. **Note:** For another way to group by opinion or interest, see **Pick Your Spot**.

Pick Your Spot (Corners)

Social skills: Vocalization, groups by interest or opinion

Group size: 4–6
Note: By having children write down responses ahead of time, they will stay on task better and get to their places quicker. You can see where they're headed and direct them to the right corner.

Directions: Pose a question or topic with four answers or subtopics and have each child select which of the four would be their choice. Have them write it down and go to the corner of the room where that topic or answer is displayed. This is a quick way to get children with similar interests together to do further study, share opinions, or become roving reporters to teach the rest of the class.
Note: For another way to group children by interest or opinion see **Line-Ups**.

Line-Ups

Social skills: Vocalization, probing for information, sharing reasons for answer

Group size: Whole class or spit in half for two lines

Note: This works best in probing an answer or problem with a range of opinions.

Directions: Create a masking tape line on your classroom floor divided into three categories; yes/ maybe/no, always/sometimes/never, etc. Pose a question or situation. Have the children write down their answer on small slips of paper. Then have them line up on the line that nearest matches their opinion. Once they're on the line, you can use the information by having them discuss with their immediate group their reasons for choosing that answer or leave their paper markers in place and go back to their desks to look and compare how many are in each section and make a class opinion graph. Some classroom teachers have developed lively discussions by having the children pair with members from other sections to discuss why they thought differently. The line can remain in place to be used later.

Stand and Share

Social skills: Speak clearly, listen actively, participate, time limit

Group size: 2–4

Directions: As in Study Group, teams ready themselves on a specific topic. Teams or members within each team number off. When the teacher calls a number, all the team members must stand and be ready to answer the question. As you call the numbers, that team or member answers the questions and sits down. This is good for an oral quiz or checking problems where all members need to know the information.

CLASSROOM MANAGEMENT CHARTS AND BUTTONS

These materials will help you define, display, and reinforce social lessons.

Social Skills T-Chart

To use: Enlarge and reproduce full-page or poster-size. Write the social skill to be learned in the top section as you discuss its importance. Have your classes brainstorm how it looks when children are using that skill, as well as how it sounds when it's happening. This gives the children a solid basis for modeling and monitoring their social behavior. Display it prominently and refer to it often. Laminate and save. Use the chart whenever that skill is being emphasized.

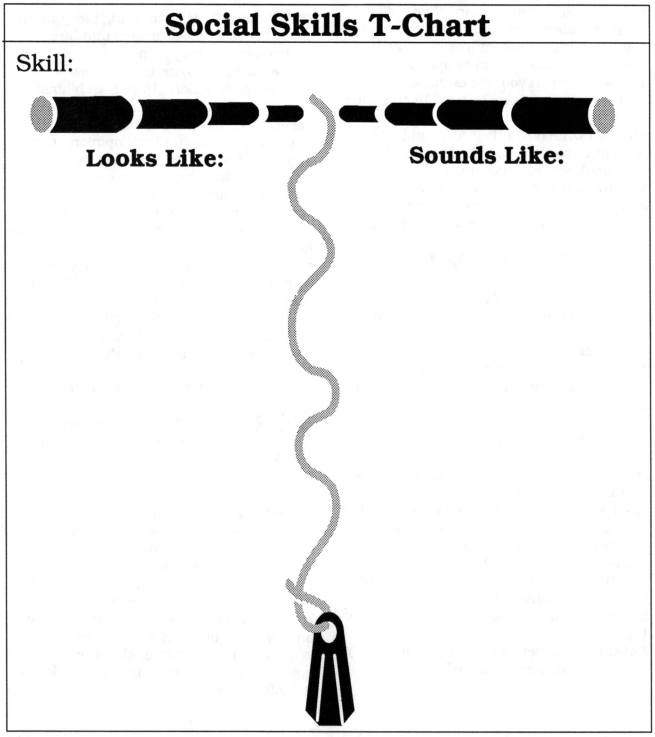

Social Skills T-Chart

Skill:

Looks Like: Sounds Like:

PRAISE WORDS

To use: In order to increase the kind and frequency of encouraging words in the classroom, brainstorm suggestions and write them in open areas within the design.
Keep them on display. As you hear others, add them to the chart with plenty of praises of your own.

Talk to others as you would have them talk to you.

Note: For a class with ingrained negative habits, it may also be helpful to put up a list of TABOO or OFF-LIMITS sayings. These can be placed on another chart with a line through them or the title "COOPERATIVE NO-NOs!"

DISCUSSION STRIPS

To use: Reproduce the strips you will use on as many different colors of paper as there are members of each team. Each student gets appropriate strips to use during group discussions. Whenever a student contributes, a strip is "spent." Discussion goes on until all have used their strips. This keeps all members contributing equally, and aware of *how* they are responding. **Note:** Younger groups may need practice in many of these modes before it comes naturally to them, so start simply. Have each child bring an envelope from home to store the strips in for later use.

Answer a Question.	Ask a Question.
Check for Understanding.	Encourage Your Group.
Give a Praise Word.	Give an Idea.
Keep Your Group on Task.	Paraphrase.
Respond to an Idea.	Summarize Progress.

EVALUATION TOOLS

TEACHER OBSERVATION FORM

To use: When your groups are working, use this form as you circulate, observe, and record their progress. Be sure to write quotes and repeat them to further reinforce and model behavior during and after the activity.

Teacher Observation Chart

Skill: _____

GROUP	STUDENTS	COMMENTS

K-W-L CHART

To use: Have the children discuss an upcoming topic and fill in questions for the K, W, and L sections. Reproduce full-page size for use in the small groups to focus learning or poster-size as a whole-class exercise to introduce a topic.

K= What I KNOW about: _____.
W= What I would like to find out: _____.
L= What I have LEARNED: _____.

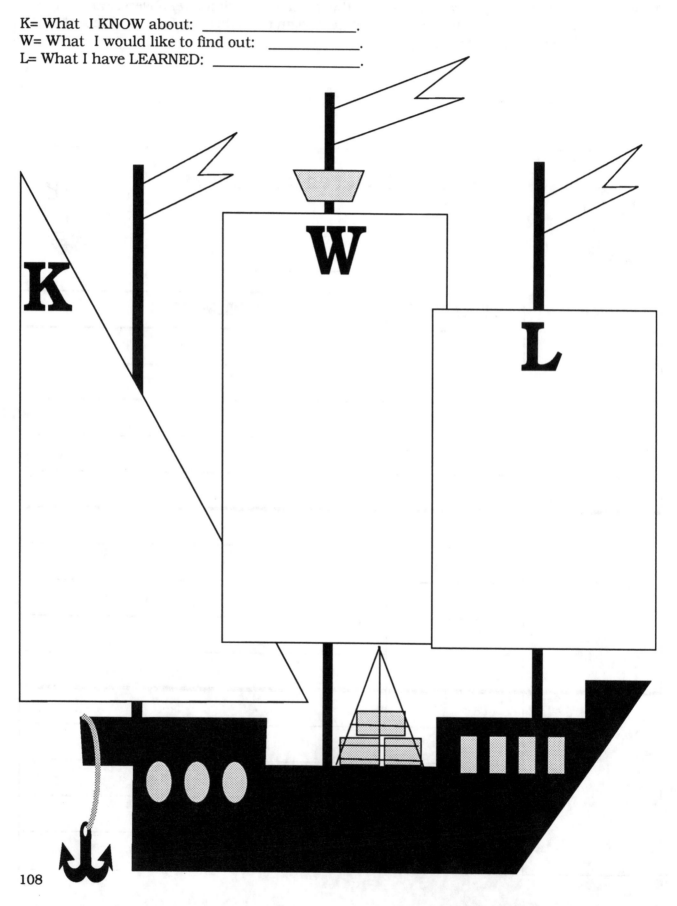

ROLE BUTTONS

To use: Reproduce on sturdy oaktag and cut out. When children are doing group work, it may help them to have a visual reminder of their group job. Use those applicable to the activity and supply them to the groups. You will also find it easier to check if students are performing as they should because you can see at a glance what each member's role is within the group.

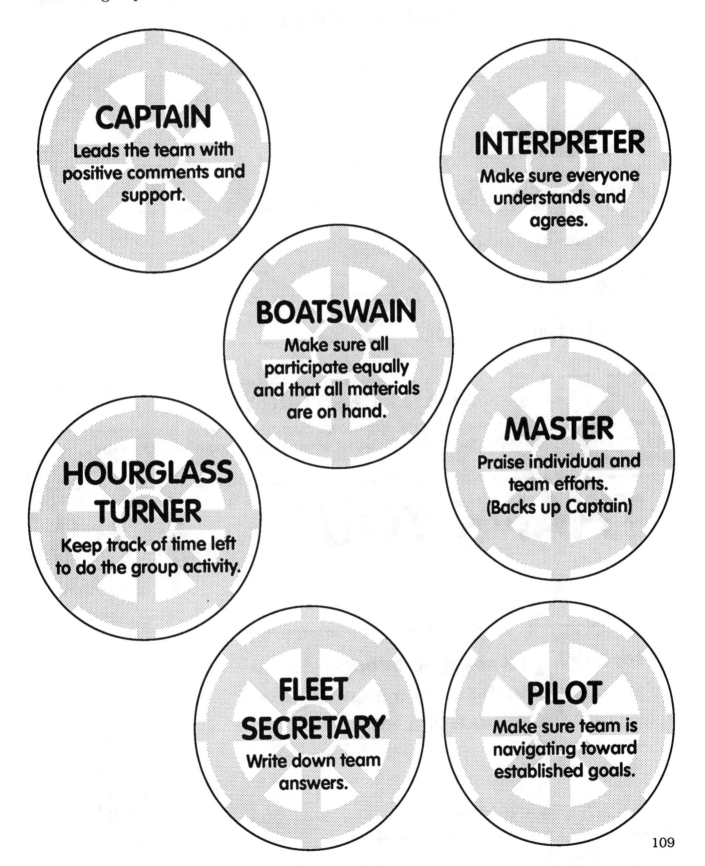

CAPTAIN
Leads the team with positive comments and support.

INTERPRETER
Make sure everyone understands and agrees.

BOATSWAIN
Make sure all participate equally and that all materials are on hand.

MASTER
Praise individual and team efforts. (Backs up Captain)

HOURGLASS TURNER
Keep track of time left to do the group activity.

FLEET SECRETARY
Write down team answers.

PILOT
Make sure team is navigating toward established goals.

GROUP EVALUATION FORM

To use: Take a few minutes after an activity for teams to evaluate their progress. The group form should be agreed upon by members, filled in, and initialed by all. The form will be helpful when groups are having problems and be able to spot areas needing improvement.

How Are We Doing?

Group: _____ Date: _____

Because: *Initial:*

1. We sailed ahead. _____ _____

2. We reached our goal. _____ _____

3. We got off course. _____ _____

4. We crashed and sank. _____ _____

5. We had smooth sailing. _____ _____

AWARD CERTIFICATE

To use: When you see groups working and accomplishing goals, give them a visual reminder of their progress. Groups can earn them, barter them, display them with team pride, or use toward whole-class goals.

THANK YOU,

_____

for helping us navigate through stormy seas to make this class a friendly place to explore and learn!

signed: _____

date: _____

SELECTED BIBLIOGRAPHY

Many materials were used in preparation of this book. The following list should be used as a starting point. Your local librarian will help you find other appropriate materials.

The Age of Discovery by Pierre Miquel (Silver Burdett Company, 1978)

The Discoverers, the Living Past (Arco Publishing, Inc., 1979)

The Expeditions of Cortés by Nigel Hunter (The Boatwright Press, 1990)

Explorers A New True Book by Dennis B. Fradin (Children's Press, 1984)

Explorers and Mapmakers by Peter Ryan (Lodestar Books, E. P. Dutton, 1989)

Explorers, The Silver Burdett Color Library by Keith Lye (Silver Burdett Company, 1983)

God, Gold, and Glory Encyclopedia of Exploration, Vol. 4 by Nicholas Hordern (Aldus Books Limited, 1971)

The Great Age of Exploration, Encyclopedia of Discovery and Exploration by Duncan Castlereagh (Aldus Books Limited, 1971)

The Great Atlas of Discovery by Neil Grant (Alfred A. Knoph, 1992)

Great Lives: Exploration by Milton Lomask (Charles Scribner's Sons, 1988)

Henry Hudson, Arctic Explorer and North American Adventurer by Isaac Asimov and Elizabeth Kaplan (Gareth Stevens Children's Books, 1991)

Illustrated Atlas of the World in the Age of Discovery, 1453-1763 by W. D. Townson (Warwick Press, 1981)

Maps and Globes by Jack Knowlton (Thomas Y. Crowell, 1988)

The Renaissance, The Living Past (Arco Publishing, Inc. 1979)

Ships and Seafarers, Tales of Ships and the Men Who Sailed Them by Erik Abramson (Silver Burdett Company, 1980)

Timespan Explorers by Tim Healey (Silver Burdett Company, 1980)

What's In a Map? by Sally Cartwright (Coward, McCann and Geoghegan, Inc., 1974)

COOPERATIVE LEARNING REFERENCES

Circles of Learning, Cooperation in the Classroom by David W. Johnson, Roger T. Johnson, Edythe Johnson Holubec, Patricia Roy (Association for Supervision and Curriculum Development, 1984)

Cooperative Learning: Getting Started by Susan Ellis and Susan Whalen (Scholastic, Inc., 1990)

Cooperative Learning Lessons for Little Ones by Lorna Curan (Resource for Teachers, 1990)

INDEX